Naturally Small

Teaching and Learning in the Last One-Room Schools

by

Stephen A. Swidler, Ph.D.

INFORMATION AGE PUBLISHING

80 Mason Street • Greenwich, Connecticut 06830 • www.infoagepub.com

Library of Congress Cataloging-in-Publication Data

Swidler, Stephen A. (Stephen Andrew)
  Naturally small : teaching and learning in the last one-room schools /
by Stephen A. Swidler.
      p. cm.
  Includes bibliographical references.
  ISBN 1-59311-122-3 (pbk.) – ISBN 1-59311-123-1 (hardcover)
  1. Rural schools–Nebraska–Case studies. 2. Effective
teaching–Nebraska–Case studies. I. Title.
  LC5147.N33S95 2004
  371'.009782'091734–dc22

                                                    2004003157

Printed in the United States of America

CONTENTS

1. Re-Bunking the One-Teacher School: Our Future in Our Past?   *1*

2. Why Consider One-Teacher Schools?   *7*

3. Two Modern One-Teacher Schools in Rural Nebraska   *15*

4. Getting Through Academic Life at Bighand School   *33*

5. Learning to Think at Upper Rill School   *59*

6. A Critical Comparison of Bighand and Upper Rill Schools   *97*

7. One-Teacher Schools, School Size and Reform   *113*

CHAPTER 1

RE-BUNKING THE ONE-TEACHER SCHOOL

Our Future in Our Past?

Joseph Featherstone (1984) writes that we are the United States of Amnesia. Our national culture is remarkably forgetful in general and in school matters in particular. We tend to neglect our own educational past, Featherstone tells us, as we grope along in present day school reform. The American penchant for self-reinvention seems to offer us license to willfully ignore the institutions in which we have historically invested so much but which also consistently let us down. Mass schooling for all children, a grand achievement in human equality by any standard, has been attained through a reified institutional organization, the "factory" model of schooling that has normalized failure and has spawned youth cultures that are troubling indeed. Deborah Meier (2000) notes that this kind of schooling has contributed to a crisis of relationship between youth and society, a crisis that a democracy should not tolerate. The large, graded school—symbol of our public commitment to and success in socializing American youth into the republic—has generated no shortage of criticism and a great deal of failure. McDermott and Varenne (1999) go so far as to call school failure, especially for marginalized children, among America's greatest cultural achievements. We have plenty of reason to want to forget our

Naturally Small: Teaching and Learning in the Last of the One-Room Schools, pages 1–5
Copyright © 2004 by Information Age Publishing
All rights of reproduction in any form reserved.

educational past and to just look ahead, for there never was a good old days in American schooling.

Yet this willed ignorance is troublesome at a number of levels. For one, it represents an ahistoricism that is distressing generally. When we despise our past and the horrible things we have done to one another in the name of achieving a country, Richard Rorty (2000) indicates that we can choose from among three paths. We can opt out altogether and commit suicide; we can engage in ceaseless self-hatred and constant recrimination that we can really do no good; or we can commit ourselves to living so as to make sure horrible things never happen again. The first two are self-destructive and justify a withdrawal from the world. The last urges us to forge ahead thoughtfully into a world of uncertainty. We cannot make such a commitment without some sense of where we have been, a knowledge of where we have gone wrong and how we have treated each other horribly. At the risk of sounding trite, this means learning from our past, not simply discarding it because of its awfulness. For school matters this would seem to entail the thoughtful criticism needed to create humane institutions that continue to be charged with bringing young people into our nation and the larger human community through a world of ideas.

At another level, perhaps there is yet something to learn from institutions that we seem to have forgotten or at least relegate to the junk pile of American educational innovations gone wrong. And that is the concern of this book. We currently have a modern rendering of a traditional genre of public schooling that we currently fail to see, use, and learn from: the rural, one-teacher school. While these schools are diminishing in number, they endure in corners of contemporary rural America and remain part of our educational landscape. When America began significant consolidation of its country schools over seventy years ago, commanders of the educational regime assumed that increased institutional size, grade level differentiation and especially economies of scale were unambiguous evidence of progress (Leight & Rhinehart, 1992). In America, bigger must be better, the old faith went. Does not common sense tell us that large scale efficiency and effectiveness go hand in hand? However, one important strain of contemporary school reform emphasizes some other, less trumpeted common sense: that students can benefit academically and socially from small, intimate, human-sized communities. This gives us pause to reconsider the old, enduring faith in school bigness.

This book takes that pause to document and compare the social organization and academic arrangement of two remaining modern, public one-teacher schools in rural Nebraska. Bighand and Upper Rill Schools are located in the rolling prairies of eastern Nebraska and are by all indications thriving institutions. The schools are situated in similar farming communities and enroll similar children. Neither school stands as educational intervention, derived from reform concerns in size. Ironically, both of these small schools stand far removed from reform consciousness, in both the minds of reformers and in the minds of the people who inhabit them. Simply put, they are *naturally occurring* small institutions, historical residue of westward expansion, white settlement and nineteenth century schooling. Each school's teacher does what comes naturally to her or him. My question is simply: How do the teachers in these small schools manage to teach? By asking this question, I am concerned with how the teachers and students in their respective schools organize themselves and "do school" that is small is scale. If school size is emerging as some important variable in student achievement and school improvement, and smallness is some key to that variable, then it stands to reason that one-teacher schools have something to tell us afterall. As Mrs. Hoffman, Bighand School's teacher, said wryly after I informed her that school smallness is grabbing the interest of some school reformers, "Well, we've had small all along."

I spent two years gathering data in these schools to create ethnographic case studies of teaching. This book presents the findings of that research. My specific concern in this study is for the relationship of the small scale structure to the organization of teaching in Bighand and Upper Rill Schools. My interest is in that special relationship that is unique to teaching: the coordination of students, their teacher and the subject matter that brings them together (Hawkins, 1974). Since these case studies are ethnographic, they concern themselves with the rather ordinary ways in which instruction is co-constructed by the teachers and students and how each teacher understands the nature of his and her work within the small scale context. These two schools I present are quintessentially rural institutions. However, my concerns are beyond rural education; the issue of school smallness cuts across traditional urban-rural divisions. But I cannot disregard the larger settings. I consider the rural community context in which the schools reside because each has particular symbolic a relationship to its community and this relationship, in turn, shapes the kinds of instruction that take place in each. This relationship is obscure and, therefore, deeply rural in the sense of the community influences. In the case of Bighand school, traditional community expectations of the teacher and the one-teacher institution are profoundly implicated in Mrs. Hoffman's practice. In the case of Upper Rill School, Teacher Will has learned to manage and effectively resist them.

What I uncovered in my time in these schools in the 1998–1999 and 1999–2000 academic years are two teachers who, despite the similarity of their schools' communities and students, engage in remarkably different teaching practices. Bighand's School's Mrs. Hoffman creates an especially efficient form of traditional, conservative teaching that echoes strongly the old country school recitation. She defines the goals of her work as ensuring that students "keep up" with their "town school" counterparts and that they "be ready" for the middle and secondary schools in which they eventually enroll. Her teaching is thus organized around "getting through" a standardized curriculum. Will Tomlinson, or "Teacher Will", as the students call him, sees his work as encouraging his students "to think" and has created a conversation-based pedagogy to achieve this. For both teachers the school size and rural circumstance inevitably play into what they believe they can and cannot do in their teaching practices. For one teacher the school presents limitations; for the other opportunity.

Observing academic life in these schools left me with a string of questions that I explore in this book. How do these teachers manage to teach and how is it that both the form and content of instruction are so remarkably different? How can two teachers, who both treat educational reforms with indifference, if not contempt, come to such remarkably different conclusions about their roles and the purpose of an education? What might we learn from Mrs. Hoffman and Teacher Will about making small-scale schooling happen? By exploring these questions we might acquire some insight that can inform current reform efforts to scale down our large schools.

While the primary audience for this book is teachers, teacher educators and education policymakers, it is my hope that others, such as parents, might pick up this book and see some images of schooling that are both familiar and strange to them. There is a large corpus of oral history on one-room schools, of which Leight and Rhinehart's (1992) *Country School Memories* is an elegant example and published by Greenwood Press. Along with these, and scores of journalistic accounts that appear in the popular press, some readers may see the continuities of curriculum and instruction in country schools past and present. Some may even see traces of their own schooling in Mrs. Hoffman's practice, teaching that has many traditional elements of recitation pedagogy that was (and, as I theorize, is) present in rural *and* urban schools. Some may be surprised to see that such practices are still in place and, like me, come to gain some sense of what school was like in these uniquely American institutions decades ago. We have every reason to infer that Mrs. Hoffman is richly immersed in a country school teaching tradition. Therefore, as we look at her work we are looking into the past. Others, also like me, may become captivated with how Teacher Will has decided, with no prompting or external incentive, to take on teaching that seeks age integration and that is conversation-based. We have many reasons to suspect that his school setting presents him with an opportunity to wonder about and, more importantly, risk trying on new forms of teaching. Some of Will's practices are consonant with the adventurous instruction some K–12 reformers call for. In short, it is my hope that the portraits of instruction I present here can offer readers something to think with as we consider what it takes to improve school life for our own and other people's children. In the process, we might capture, in the words of Nebraska filmmaker Joel Geyer (1995), a glimpse "of our future in this remaining piece of our past."

PLAN OF THE BOOK

In Chapter 2 I frame the problem of studying instructional practices of one-teacher schools within the context the emerging reform movement in school size and I outline my research methodology and the study's limitations. After I introduce Bighand and Upper Rill Schools in Chapter 3, I present two ethnographic case studies of the organization of teaching in the schools. In Chapter 4 for Bighand School and in Chapter 5 for Upper Rill School, I offer "thick description" of teaching practices and how academic life is generally organized. I also examine in these chapters specific instances of instruction that are representative of the whole of teaching at these schools and illustrate the complexity of teaching interactions. Chapter 6 then offers a critical comparison of the teaching practices. In this chapter I make some statement as to the symbolic and concrete functions of the respective teaching practices and what they represent for both the insiders to the schools and communities and to outsiders, like me, who are ultimately interested in learning what we can learn from these schools as we seek to improve the academic life of children. The last chapter ends with my comment on what this study holds for change in instruction in small scale schooling and for rural education reforms.

REFERENCES

Featherstone, J. (1984). Forward, In Herbert Kohl (Ed.), *Growing minds: On becoming a teacher.* New York: Harper Torchbooks.

Geyer. J. (Producer/Director). (1995). *Last of the one-room schools.* Lincoln, NE: Nebraska Educational Television.

Hawkins, D. (1974). I, thou, and it. In D. Hawkins (Ed.), *The informed vision: Essays on learning and human nature* (pp. 48–62). New York: Agathon Press.

Leight, R. L., & Rhienhart, A. D. (1992). Revisiting Americana: One-room school in retrospect. *The Educational Forum,* 56(2), 135–151.

Meier, D. (2000). *Will standards save public education?* Boston: Beacon Press

Rorty, R. (2000). American national pride. In *Achieving our country: Leftist thought in twentieth-century America.* Cambridge, MA: Harvard University Press.

Varenne, H., & McDermott, R.(1998). *Successful failure: The school America builds.* Boulder, CO: Westview Press.

CHAPTER 2

WHY CONSIDER ONE-TEACHER SCHOOLS?

RESEARCH AND REFORM: SMALL SCALE SCHOOLING

Nebraska's one-teacher schools present an opportunity to consider the growing reform concern with school size and "scaling down." School size is now indisputably an important reform issue (Ayers, Klonsky, & Lyon, 2000). Though reform interest in school size is relatively recent, research on school size reaches back to Barker and Gump's *Big School, Small School* (1964). By today's research standards, this study is rather limited. The authors did not focus on core matters of schooling, i.e., the organization and processes of curriculum, teaching and learning. Rather, Barker and Gump concentrated on extracurricular activities as indicators of student engagement in high school life. Moreover, the authors were attempting to press a psychological framework for investigation into issues that are essentially sociological, e.g., institutional organization and the structure of student experience. Despite these criticisms, *Big School, Small School* did make a profound insight: students in smaller high schools tend to have greater opportunity *and* greater motivation to become involved in school life than students in larger high schools. This indicates that it is more likely in the small high school for a student to have a place and be a legitimate member of a community. As the Barker and Gump say, no one in the small school is "redundant." This points to important sociological concerns of anomie and society. More importantly, their work points to something about the "black box" of the small school: *something* in its social configuration and social practices allows for students to

Naturally Small: Teaching and Learning in the Last of the One-Room Schools, pages 7–14
Copyright © 2004 by Information Age Publishing
All rights of reproduction in any form reserved.

have a place and to become part of the life of a school. For more contemporary concerns in research on teaching and learning in small and rural schools, this indicates potential for enhanced instructional relationships. Something in the small school can make life better for students.

Since the publication of *Big School, Small School*, a significant amount of research evidence concerned more with the core of schooling points to the importance of school size in student achievement (see Cotton, 1996; Gladden, 1998). For instance, the sophisticated work of Bryk, Lee, & Holland (1993) finds that Catholic high schools' small size strongly interacts with a number of other features that induce social and academic engagement, healthy relationships between teachers and students, increased teacher satisfaction, and a strong sense of connection and commitment to school communities.

Recent scholarship in school restructuring paints a complex picture of the conditions and outcomes of small school settings. For example, Newmann and Wehlage (1996) find reduced school and class size are necessary conditions to develop "authentic" achievement at elementary and secondary levels, that the small scale can play a role in developing academic tasks that are congruent with the work of real practitioners in the disciplines. The National Education Longitudinal Study (NELS) informs that restructured small schools strengthen teacher collaboration, facilitate coherent curricula, and subject students to higher "academic press" (Lee & Smith, 1999, 2001). NELS found that these, in turn, lead to distinct academic gains, especially for low income and minority students (Lee & Smith, 1996) who consistently and persistently experience school failure. The Consortium on Chicago School Research (Bryk, Lee, & Holland, 1993; Lee & Loeb, 2000) finds effective change more likely to occur in smaller schools, with teachers taking greater responsibility for student learning, regular debate among staff and parents about what is good for children, and facilitating a greater collaboration or "strong democracy." Combined with practitioner portraits of famous small schools, such as Central Park East Elementary and Secondary schools (e.g., Meier, 1995; Snyder, J. et al., 1992), these give us a sense of life as it might be in the small school, places of lively intellectual habits and commitments to link more democratic principles to academic achievement.

Despite the research findings, and the achievements of famous small schools, the research also indicates that small school size is no policy panacea (Raywid, 1996; Lee et al., 2000). Learning to create, sustain, and exploit small scale structures is a formidable task. Small schools may maintain conservative practices (e.g., teacher-centered and textbook-centered instruction) for what they, their teachers and their communities perceive to be sensible reasons. Change in practice may be viewed by school constituents as overly risky, unnecessary or, more pessimistically, unattainable.

Nonetheless, smallness is thoroughly implicated in robust school improvement (Clinchy, 2000). Consequently, policy scholars and reformers urge schools to "scale down" (Elmore, 1996), restructure into small, multi-age units, and create "schools-within-schools" (e.g., Darling-Hammond, 1997) so as to create the conditions and the capacity necessary to enable instructional improvement. A recent book from a major educational research publisher casts the problem in moral terms and names the creation of small schools "a simple justice" (Ayers et al., 2000).

NEGLECTING ONE-TEACHER SCHOOLS

It is not uncommon to hear those representing the "small schools movement" (typically urban) at research conferences invoke the one-room country school as inspiration for their efforts. Even some of the most realistic, and skeptical, of reformers will wistfully refer to the one-room school as some model of what they envision. There is something about the image of the school that tugs at educators' sentiments. Yet, we have little reason to believe that these schools were ever "laboratories of democracy" (Theobald, 1995) or enclaves exciting pedagogy (Cuban, 1994). The historical evidence points to the contrary, that they were rigid, authoritarian environments that valued rote memorization. More important to my concern, contemporary rural, one-teacher schools continue to be overlooked by educational researchers. Their appearance in rural educational research is limited to statistical descriptions (e.g., Muse, Hite, Randall, & Jensen, 1998). These are derived from surveys that make rather strained inferences as to the nature and quality of instruction and that characteristically conflate teaching practices with inscribed curricula. Small country schools and school districts do appear in larger quantitative studies (e.g., Fowler, 1995; Howley, 1989; Howley & Bickel, 1999). However, these ratify what we already know from other large, more powerful and sophisticated mainstream studies that are not exclusively rural: smaller is better. Published descriptive analysis research of instructional practices in contemporary small, public, rural elementary schools, and one-teacher schools in particular, is practically nonexistent.

One of the few academic treatments of public one-teacher schools is a research center monograph, derived from a dissertation, called "The Vermont Schoolmarm" (Kenny, 1990). While valuable as a historical document for its descriptive cataloging of contemporary one-room school activities and the teacher's labors in one of the few one-room schools in modern Vermont, this work remains elegiac and does not analyze instructional practices for theoretical or reform utility. DeWalt and Troxler (1989) offer an insightful analysis of the socialization function of traditional, Men-

nonite one-room schools. Their work indicates an important and complicated relationship between the schools and "old order" Mennonite
communities. But these are particularly religiously-oriented communities
and their schools are implicated in religious socialization of children. Public, country schools enjoy no such clarity of purpose. Study of these Mennonite schools can address only indirectly reform concerns with size. In short,
no published research takes a systematic look at how the public, one
teacher schools are socially organized and, more relevant to contemporary
mainstream teaching reforms, how one-teacher schools are arranged academically in relation to their small size.[1] What makes public, rural, one-
teachers schools of theoretical import and reform interest is that they are
naturally occurring instances of small-scale schooling. Their size is a function
of social and historical circumstance, not of reform intervention. They are
"just so" as rural institutions. The one-teacher school is the quintessential
rural institution (an urban one-teacher school sounds like an oxymoron)
and was initially where most children of the American prairie and Great
Plains were educated. Continuing rural depopulation and a hegemony of
economy of scale ideologies (i.e., bigger is better) have both contributed to
their widespread closure and school consolidation. The research I present
here was undertaken to look at the practices of two of the remaining public
one-teacher schools and what might be learned from them before they dis-
appear from the educational landscape altogether.

THEORETICAL AND METHODOLOGICAL
CONCERNS OF THE STUDY

In 1997, when this study was conceived, Nebraska had more living one-
teacher schools than any other state (DeWalt, 1997; Muse et al., 1998).
Combined with their absence from the research literature, I considered
this an extraordinary opportunity, especially in light of the place of school
size in educational reform. Since my interests are in Nebraska's remaining
one-teacher schools as naturally occurring instances of small scale schooling, I use a theoretical orientation and research methodology that are
appropriate to the study of sociocultural phenomena in natural settings.
The research combines the depth of ethnography with the leverage of
comparative case study (Heath, 1983). Ethnographic analysis is best suited
to attend holistically to the details and subtleties of practice in such settings, especially when insider perspective is crucial to understanding those
settings. While no school is truly "natural" (they are human-made institutions), the rural one-teacher school is, in educational and institutional
terms, not a design for change. It is in many ways a mundane cultural setting, where school constituents take for granted its meaning. They come

together to share symbols, create and coordinate rights and obligations that frame practices as a way to "do school" that is small in scale. This makes the one-teacher school susceptible to interpretive inquiry.

In data collection and analysis, this study takes a symbolic-interpretive perspective on the schools as cultural settings (Erickson, 1986). I view the practices in each school, in Geertz's (1973a) words, as "an ensemble of texts, themselves ensembles, which the anthropologist strains to read over the shoulders of those to whom they properly belong" (p. 452). In struggling to read over the shoulders of the "natives" in the schools, I assume that there is a "historically transmitted pattern of meanings embodied in symbols, a system of inherited conceptions expressed in symbolic form by means of which [people] communicate, perpetuate, and develop their knowledge about and attitudes towards life" (Geertz, 1973b, p. 89). Here, I consider, specifically, instructional practices as patterned meanings of the cultures of two small country schools. My concerns center on how practices in these traditional institutions cohere in their small and rural circumstance. The comparative case study perspective allows me to demonstrate the variation of teaching practices in schools with similar children, in similar communities in the same state and to contrast their concrete and symbolic functions.

My methodology employed long-term participant-observation, in-depth interviews, and artifact and documentary examination. Data collection included participant-observation at Bighand School and then Upper Rill Schools for the first six months of the 1998–1999 and 1999–2000 academic years. During this time I spent at least two days full days per week and made several return visits later in the school years. I attended monthly school board meetings and conducted in-depth interviews with the teachers, students, school board members, parents, administrators and community members. I endeavored especially to interview the students, individually and in groups. I conducted follow-up interviews with students, parents, the teacher and school board members, formally and informally (sometimes in telephone calls), to verify emergent assertions and to build working hypotheses about "what is going on" at the school. I also reviewed various textbooks, curriculum guides, and written school policies as documentary artifacts and symbolic tracings of what the school "means."

Though I gathered a good deal of observational data, yielding hundreds of pages of fieldnotes, and ended up with a large corpus of recorded interviews, a great amount of what I consider precious data comes from the several hundred small conversations I had with the students and the teachers during everyday school activities were taking place: sitting next to students as they worked, in musty basements during lunch, on the school grounds in games of *Andy, Andy Over* and kickball (where I was *everlasting pitcher*), and during dizzying rides on ancient country school merry-go-rounds. I spent a good deal of time writing their words in my field notebook. One Bighand student wanted to know why I spent so much time in my car in the morning and afternoons writing in my notebook. "Because I have a lousy memory," I told her. And it was to ensure that I could as accurately as possible capture their words so as to reconstitute them here as authentic indicators of their experience and understanding of life at the schools as the activities were taking place.

LIMITS OF THE STUDY

This study is bounded (Stake, 1995) by its concerns for how teaching practices and classroom interaction are co-constructed by the teachers and students of Bighand and Upper Rill Schools in the school years I observed them. I do draw out the place of the school in the imaginations of their respective community members. However, I had neither the means nor the resources to conduct extensive community studies. While I did visit and enjoy county and state archives to gain some historical background, I did not, for instance, conduct an extensive oral history of each school and of the teaching practices former students were subjected to in different eras. This would have been daunting since each school was formed in the 19th century. I paid little attention in the study to the specific politics of board activities or any larger community conflicts around the school and only as they were relevant to the teachers' practices. This study doesn't address the gendered aspects of teaching. This could conceivably be fruitful for study, especially since one of the teachers in this book is male and, therefore, an anomaly (historically country school teaching has been feminized, considered "women's work"). It would take a different form of historical review and community study to understand the role of school women in a community.

Lastly, because this study is ethnographic, examining the particulars of each school's present instructional practices, the "findings" are in no way generalizable in the conventional social science sense. In fact, the sheer contrast of, or variation in, the teaching practices in the two schools presented here would argue against seeking a general causal model of one-teacher school instructional practices. Generalizability for any qualitative research is an empirical matter, what a reader does with the particulars of what is presented in a research report. To be sure, I draw general principles that this study has for small scale school reform and rural education. But I make no claims as to the distribution of teaching practices that I witnessed in either Bighand or Upper Rill Schools, only the theoretical likelihood that their practices may or may not exist in other one-teacher schools. More importantly, I posit that school size, in and of itself has no generalizable effects. It is simply a kind of resource that can potentially enable certain forms of teaching. Any insight for reforms is gained from looking at what particular teachers do, or do not do, with the resource of smallness.

NOTE

1. By this I mean systematic qualitative research. Here, perhaps unfairly, I exclude oral history, reminiscence, memoir, autobiography and scores of journalistic accounts. To be sure, there is much to be mined in these, but none of them represent systematic inquiry into *living, contemporary,* one-teacher, public schools.

REFERENCES

Ayers, W., Klonsky, M., & Lyon, G. (Eds.). (2000). *A simple justice: The challenge of small schools.* New York: Teachers College Press.

Barker, R., & Gump, P. (1964). *Big school, small school: High school size and student behavior.* Stanford, CA: Stanford University Press.

Bryk, A., Easton, J. Q., Kerbow, D., Rollow, S. G., & Sebing, P. A. (1993). *A view from the elementary schools: The state of reform in Chicago.* Chicago: Consortium on Chicago School Research.

Bryk, A. S., Lee, V. E., & Holland, P. B. (1993). *Catholic schools and the common good.* Cambridge, MA: Harvard University. Press.

Clinchy, E. (2000). *Creating new schools: How small schools are changing American education.* New York: Teachers College Press.

Cotton, K. (1996). School size, school climate, and student performance. *School improvement research series. 10(20).* Portland, OR: Northwest Regional Educational Laboratory.

Cuban, L. (1994). *How teachers taught: Constancy and change in American classrooms.* New York: Teachers College Press.

Darling-Hammond, L. (1997). *The right to learn: A blueprint for creating schools that work.* San Francisco: Jossey-Bass.

DeWalt, M. (1997). *One-room school: Current trend in public and private education.* Winthrop University.

DeWalt, M., & Troxler, B. (1989). Old Order Mennonite one-room school: A case study. *Anthropology and Education Quarterly. 20(4),* 308–325.

Elmore, R. F. (1996). Getting down to scale with good educational practice. *Harvard Educational Review, 66(1),* 1–26.

Erickson, F. (1986). Qualitative methods. In M. C. Wittrock (Ed.), *Handbook of research on teaching.* New York: Macmillan.

Fowler, W. J. (1995). School size and student outcomes. *Advances in Educational Productivity, 5,* 3–36.

Geertz, C. (1973a). Deep play: Notes on the Balinese cockfight. *The interpretation of cultures.* New York: Basic Books.

Geertz, C. (1973b). Religion as a cultural system. *The interpretation of cultures.* New York: Basic Books.

Gladden, R. (1998). The small school movement: A review of the literature. In M. Fine & J. I. Somerville, (Eds.), *Small schools, big imaginations: A creative look at urban public schools* (pp. 113–137). Chicago: Cross City Campaign for Urban School Reform.

Heath, S. Brice. (1983). *Ways with words: Language, life, and work in communities and classrooms.* New York: Cambridge University Press.

Howley, C. (1989). Synthesis of the effects of school and district size: What research says about achievement in small schools and school districts. *Journal of Rural and Small Schools, 4*(1), 2–12.

Howley, C., & Bickel, H. (2000). The influence of scale on school performance: A multi-level extension of the Matthew Principle. *Education Policy Analysis Archives, 8*(22). Available: http://0-epaa.asu.edu.library.unl.edu:80/epaa.

Kenny, J. (1990). *The Vermont schoolmarm and the contemporary one-room schoolhouse: An ethnographic study of a contemporary one-room schoolteacher.* University of Vermont, Burlington, VT: Center for Research on Vermont.

Lee, V., & Loeb, S. (2000). School size in Chicago elementary schools: Effects on teachers' attitudes and students' achievement. *American Educational Research Journal, 37*(1), 3–31.

Lee, V., & Smith, J. B. (2001). *Restructuring high schools for equity and excellence: What works.* New York: Teachers College Press.

Lee, V., & Smith, J. B. (1999). Social support and achievement for young adolescents in Chicago: The role of academic press. *American Education Research Journal, 36,* 907–945.

Lee, V., Smerdon, B., Alfredo-Liro, C., & Brown, S. (2000). Inside large and small high schools; Curriculum and social relations. *Education and Policy Analysis, 22*(2), 147–171.

Meier, D. (1995). *The power of their ideas: lessons for America from a small school in Harlem.* Boston: Beacon Press.

Muse I, Hite, S., Randall, V., & Jensen, A. (1998). One-teacher schools in America. *Teacher Educator, 33*(3), 141–149.

Newmann, F., & Wehlage. G. G. (1996). Conclusion: Restructuring for authentic instruction. In F. Newman and Associates (Eds.), *Authentic achievement: Restructuring schools for intellectual quality.* San Francisco: Jossey-Bass Publishers.

Raywid, M.A. (1996). The Wadleigh Complex: A dream that soured. In B. Boyd, B. Crowson, & H. Mawhinney, (Eds.), *The politics of education and then new institutionalism: Reinventing the American school* (pp. 101–114). Philadelphia: Falmer.

Snyder, J., Lieberman, A., MacDonald, M. B., & Goodwin, A. L. (1992). *Makers of meaning in a learning-centered school: A case study of Central Park East 1 Elementary School.* National Center for Restructuring Education, School and Teaching: New York.

Stake, R. (1995). *The art of case study research.* Thousand Oaks, CA: Sage.

Theobald, P. (1995). *Call school: Rural education in the Midwest to 1918.* Carbondale: Southern Illinois University Press.

CHAPTER 3

TWO MODERN ONE-TEACHER SCHOOLS IN RURAL NEBRASKA

This chapter notes the unique features of Nebraska school districting and legislation that has permitted the state to maintain the largest number of public one-teacher schools in the U.S. The chapter then introduces Big-hand and Upper Rill Schools for the years I collected data, the students, their families and the communities in which they reside. It offers basic information on the rural and agricultural contexts in which the schools are both situated. It also describes the biographies of the two teachers, as these are extraordinarily important to the contexts of instruction.

NEBRASKA'S REMAINING ONE-TEACHER SCHOOLS

Nebraska continues to have more living one-teacher schools than any other state. From the most recent aggregated, national data we have on one-room schools (DeWalt, 1997; Muse, Hite, Randall, & Jensen, 1998), I estimate that there were around 350 remaining one-teacher schools in the U.S. at the time I initiated data collection for this study in 1998. In 1984 there were 749 of these schools (DeWalt, 1997). In 1931 there were 143,391 one-room schools and 25,341 a quarter of a century later (Leight

Naturally Small: Teaching and Learning in the Last of the One-Room Schools, pages 15–31
Copyright © 2004 by Information Age Publishing
All rights of reproduction in any form reserved.

& Rhienhart, 1992). In the 1998–1999 school year, Nebraska had 125 one-teacher schools and in 1999–2000, there were exactly 100.[1]

The one-teacher schools in Nebraska are variants of "Class One" school districts. These districts are classified kindergarten through eighth grade only (i.e., those that have no high school). This does not mean they do not close or consolidate. In the 1998–1999 school year there were 320 Class One school districts in the state and in 1999–2000 there were 278. Until 2002, there were state incentive monies for consolidation or what is euphemistically called "merger." And calls from various interest groups for their dismantling and consolidation are perennial political sport in Nebraska.[2]

Because their existence is a matter of state districting policies, Class One schools have a statutory right to exist; to eliminate entirely the remaining one-teacher schools in the state would require a legislative act on school redistricting.[3] These schools have between one and twelve teachers. The one-teacher schools, like all Class Ones, comprise their own districts with their own three-person school boards. This is not common knowledge, even among educators in the state, and strikes many as odd or "primitive" as one Lincoln, Nebraska elementary principal told me derisively.

Closing the Class One schools thus remains a local matter, subject to local political decision making. There are a myriad of reasons that the schools close, or their board and communities think they should close. An aging population, a general rural population decline, ongoing tax struggles involving a state-mandated property tax lid, a convoluted and perceived inequitable state aid distribution system, professionalization of teaching (i.e., finding and retaining qualified teachers and providing salaries for credentialed professionals), social and political pressure from nearby rural and non-rural school districts, and economies of scale ideologies all contribute to decisions to close the small, Class One schools.[4] But, at present, the decision to maintain or close Class One schools, and, therefore, one-teacher schools, remains a local matter; any one's closing is subject to the discretion of its local school board or, in some cases where a school board does not want to take on the responsibility of that decision, to a vote of a district's registered voters.

Of importance to the current configuration of Class One school districts are school affiliation polices. In the mid-1980s, as part of a state-wide effort to equalize property taxes, rural landowners were required to declare their association with a school district. Their school property taxes would go to that district. If they chose a Class One district, landowners were also required to select a high school and a percentage of their school taxes would go to that high school. Later in 1990, this high school portion of the law was modified and each Class One school was required to formally "affiliate" with one or more high schools or to become a subset of a Class Six (high school only) district. This led to a patchwork for some districts, with a good deal of non-contiguous land and predictable tax conflicts (e.g., one neighboring district taxing at a lower rate, etc.). In this policy, each of the affiliated high school districts' school boards have budgetary oversight since school revenues now flow through these districts to the Class Ones.

Unsurprisingly this presents an awkward political situation for the Class Ones whose own school boards have to work with these affiliated boards in setting school budgets. And it is not unwarranted to suspect that the state affiliation policy as it was originally conceived was a not so cryptic effort to push for consolidation. The Class One budgets effectively represent a potential revenue source for the larger affiliated district (though they would have to absorb the Class One students and per pupil costs). However, legally and morally these larger districts cannot strangle the schools financially because they still must budget for teacher salaries, equipment, textbooks and per pupil enrollments. The affiliated districts' superintendents have varying degrees of good will toward these schools (as I note in Chapters 4 and 5). While the superintendents of the affiliated high school districts can, and often do, campaign, sometimes strenuously, for Class One closure, an affiliated district does not have the legal authority to close them down. This is significant to the extent that Bighand School affiliates with three different high schools in three different districts. This is less significant for Upper Rill School, though the superintendent of its single affiliated district is very public about his desire to see the school close. Each school has resisted closure and consolidation.

BIGHAND SCHOOL IN 1998–1999

Bighand School is located in the rolling prairie of eastern Nebraska, where corn, soybeans and winter wheat cover the landscape during the growing season. The school is situated three miles from the unincorporated village of Johnville (pop. 170), seven miles from the town of Sparta (pop. 1,700), and twelve miles from the county seat, Riverview (pop. 6,000), which has a small industrial base. It is literally "in the country," on a dirt state highway. "Not enough rich people live on it to be paved," one parent remarked. It is located on a hill crest and approaching Bighand School from any direction one sees a bland, utterly conventional building. Constructed in 1981, the current 25' × 40' building is one story, with white aluminum siding, a storage shed, an old water pump, a detached tornado cellar, two swing sets and a small merry-go-round. County archives indicate that the school was founded in 1868, a year after Nebraska became a state. Consequently Bighand remains one of the oldest living schools in the state. Like a great portion of eastern Nebraska and western Iowa, the region in and around

Bighand School was homesteaded and settled in the nineteenth century primarily by German immigrants. The vast majority of the registered voters, as well as all of the students and the teacher at Bighand School, bear German surnames attesting to this historical-cultural backdrop. It took the name Bighand sometime in the 1880s, apparently from the name of the farmer whose original homestead property sat next to the school and who served on the school board.[5] In a county that encompasses nineteen separate school districts, nine of which are Class One, Bighand is one of the five remaining one-teacher schools.

Bighand School district encompasses no population centers in a largely agricultural county. U.S. Department of Agriculture data indicate that in 1997 there were just over 550 farms in the county. Many of the district's residents are retired farmers. The land in the district is presently farmed by family farmers or tenant farmers, with a small number of incorporated and consolidated farms. The 1998 school census indicates that there are 66 residents in the Bighand School district and seventeen school-age (K–8) children, with eight of those attending Bighand School. The district has weathered decades of school district reorganization and witnessed neighboring rural districts close and consolidate. Once composed of 10 square miles, Bighand district now includes approximately 25 square miles, some of which is non-contiguous. The current Bighand district configuration is the effect of landowners' affiliation choices.

The political and social boundaries of the community are effectively defined by the school district. Because there are no economic or formal social centers in the district itself, constituents take up shopping and church in the surrounding towns and villages. At least one parent in each of this year's school families is employed in one of these neighboring towns or villages. One parent referred to the school as the "capital" of the community. With no tax advantage in retaining a separate rural school district and no high school, the preservation of the Bighand district has seemed peculiar to many in the county. In 1981, the regional electric utility's newsletter sounded a note of bemusement that while the rest of the state's one-teacher schools were closing and consolidating, Bighand's school board proudly paid $50,000 to replace the deteriorating, 100 year-old building with one that "boosts such amenities as a full basement, fluorescent lighting, a 30-gallon electric hot water heater, an electric cook range, and a new 20-kilowatt electric furnace." A Bighand student, quoted in Riverview's newspaper, said enthusiastically of the new building, "It's bigger, more attractive and it has a drinking fountain and indoor plumbing!" The old building is now a fertilizer storage shed on a farm a few miles north of the school.

Bighand Students This Year

This year Bighand School has twelve students, spanning kindergarten through 8th grade. Table 3.1 shows the children and their grade levels. Eight of these children reside in the school district.[6] The four whose families do not reside are "option" students. The State of Nebraska statutorily allows "option enrollment," where parents can place their children in any public school in the state as long as they can provide transportation to that school, there is room at a school, and school desegregation plans are not compromised. Samuel, Christine and Andrew are from Johnville. Loretta is from Sparta. Though the parents of these students have different reasons for "optioning" their children into Bighand School, they express a common reservation toward large, graded schools of the Johnville-Sparta Consolidated School District (all use the terms "fear" or "afraid"). They indicate a belief that in a country school discipline is enforced and children get personal attention from the teacher. *Every* parent and community member with whom I spoke or interviewed uses the phrase "one on one" to describe a major benefit of country schooling. A presumption of personal attention and a concern for surveillance and discipline is part of a larger set of community values discussed in Chapter 6.

Table 3.1. Students at Bighand School, 1998–99

Grade	Student
K	Haley
K	Andrew*
1st	Samuel*
2nd	Christine*
2nd	Richard
2nd	David
5th	Kimberly
6th	Daisy
6th	Deborah
8th	Mary
8th	Loretta*
8th	Molly

*children who reside in another district and are "option enrollment" students.

The parents of Bighand's students are mostly skilled laborers and limited to a high school education (see Table 3.2). Only Mary and Deborah's parents and Loretta's stepfather are college educated. None of these families considers itself poor. While they never refer to each other as wealthy, I have, though, overheard hushed, reproachful comments as to Loretta's mother's displays of wealth in her clothing, hairstyle, dress and automobiles. If there is any class consciousness, or resentment, it is half-buried or ill-defined (I once heard Loretta call Kimberly "a rich kid" when her own family's income is clearly and demonstrably higher than any other family's in the school). Of this year's students, Haley and Molly, Christine and Samuel, David and Kimberly, Mary and Deborah are siblings. In other words, seventy-five percent of the school is made up of four families.

Table 3.2. Bighand Parent Occupations and Educational Levels

	Parent Occupation		Parent Education (highest level achieved)	
Student (grade)	Mother	Father	Mother	Father
Haley (K) Molly (8th)	Stay at home	Mining laborer	High School	High School
Andrew (K)	Fast food assistant manager	Factory laborer	High School	High School
Samuel (1st) Christine (2nd)	Stay at home	Farm laborer	High School	High School
Richard (2nd)	Factory laborer	Out of state (divorced)	High School	unknown
David (2nd) Kimberly (5th)	Seamstress	Power company supervisor	High School	High School
Daisy (6th)	Lumber company clerk	Meat packing laborer (divorced)	High School	High School
Deborah (6th) Mary (8th)	Social worker	Farmer, feed store owner	Undergraduate University	Undergraduate University
Loretta (8th)	Stay at home	Optometrist (step-father)	High School	Post-graduate

Ruralness Intimacy at School

The school these children inhabit has a "rural" quality. In the area it is commonly referred to as "the one-room school north of Johnville." In addition to "being in the country," the school board president and secretary farm for a living. The school is deeded on a corner of the board president's farm. Most of the families and the teacher have some substantial connection to agriculture in their family histories. For example, Haley and Molly's father farmed until a decade earlier when he calculated the economic risk was too great and went to work for a prosperous mining company. Daisy's mother "grew up a farm kid" not far from the school. Furthermore, the teacher, parents, school board members, and students make regular and firm distinctions between "country" and "town" schools (small and multi-grade vs. large and graded) and imply the inferiority of the latter. Though only one of the school's families currently farms for a living, Deborah and Mary's, the location, history and community sentiment give the school a decidedly "rural" flavor.

This rural flavor is accompanied by a peculiar intimacy. Walking into Bighand School at almost any given time during school hours, one will see students preoccupied with preparing for their recitations with the teacher. With its dingy linoleum floor, blond pine book cases, and white painted walls, the school appears quiet and emotionally remote to outsiders like me. Students display insouciance, and sometimes harshness, toward one another in their classroom and playground interactions and in their interviews with me. For instance, Daisy says to me that she "can't stand the younger kids" and snaps to Samuel, "Sit down, be quiet, and stop bothering me" when he squirms in his chair. Mary accuses Kimberly of stealing things from coat pockets and backpacks and calls her "stuck up." Loretta refers to David as a "brat." Defending her brother, Kimberly returns the sentiment and tells that Loretta is "nothing but trouble." And Mrs. Hoffman regularly harangues Richard to "sit down, get to work or otherwise you will lose your recess," and bluntly tells a crying Deborah that "the older girls pick on you because you sometimes ask for it."

But the apparent coolness these people hold toward one another belies certain important facts. Apart from Richard, a newcomer this year, and Loretta, who option enrolled in the middle of her sixth grade year, Bighand School is the only school these students have ever attended. Moreover, since she is in her eleventh year at the school, Mrs. Hoffman is the only teacher they have known. Consequently, the teacher and students have a protracted familiarity with each other. Molly reports that she and the other older students regard Mrs. Hoffman as a cantankerous "aunt," and the students frequently call her "Mrs. H." This represents an oblique intimacy that Alan Peshkin (1979/1994) describes as knowing, and being known by, others through long-term, mundane interaction characteristic of small and rural communities. At Bighand School the students have extensive knowledge of each other through their own everyday interactions, what their brothers and sisters say to them about other students, what they hear from their parents about other students and their families, and so on. When one is very familiar with others, and one's schoolwork is centered around working quietly, strenuously and individually on textbook and workbook assignments, sometimes there is not that much to cheerfully talk about. And there are some things one wants to keep to oneself in such an intimate environment. The people at Bighand School have simply, to paraphrase Lerner & Lowe (1959), grown accustomed to each other's faces. Though they may not say often that they like each other, the students know each other very well and are regular parts of each other's lives.

The Teacher: Mrs. Hoffman

Mrs. Hoffman is in her 11th year of teaching at Bighand. She returned to teaching not long after the sudden death of her husband. Now in her early sixties, she was originally educated in what was then a state Normal School in the 1950s. After completing a relatively short course in teacher education, she received a provisional teaching certificate at the age of eighteen with the stipulation that she ultimately complete a two-year teacher certification program. She took up her first teaching job in a country school for four years. Like many women of her generation, she left teaching to marry and raise children. Between those early years and her 11 year tenure at Bighand, she has worked as a fraternity house mother, a social service provider, and a seamstress at a retail clothiers. She still works part-time at a clothing retailer in Riverview to make ends meet (the school board pays her less than $19,000 annually). Mrs. Hoffman returned to that same Normal School in the early 1980s, which had become a four year college, to obtain her certification.

Mrs. Hoffman calls herself "country schooled." She tells that when she transferred from a small country school to a village high school, with a graduating class of 15, she experienced "culture shock." Culturally and educationally speaking, she has deep roots in country schooling and in the region: she was born and raised in a small town 30 miles south of the school and in the same county; she currently lives in Sparta; she went to country schools; she recalls vividly a grandmother who taught in country schools ("I learned everything from her"); before school starts in the mornings she ordinarily and amicably talks with the school aide (the board president's wife) about mutual friends and acquaintances in the community; and she had coursework and practica on country schooling in her early teacher education at a state Normal School. The previous board secretary (Molly and Haley's mother) indicated that Mrs. Hoffman was selected from a pool of 30 applicants because the board assumed she understood "schools like these" and country children. In Mrs. Hoffman's words, "teaching in a country school is in my blood."

UPPER RILL SCHOOL IN 1999–2000

Like Bighand School Upper Rill School is located in the rich farming prairie of the eastern half Nebraska. The school is situated between four communities and school districts of various sizes. It is located 10 miles from a large town, United; 5 miles from the village Dark Glen, whose elementary school is consolidated with the schools of Portage, another 5 miles directly to the west; 12 miles from the town of Benefit; 6 miles from the village of Nickels.[7] Like Bighand, it is literally in the country, on a dirt road that is a 100 mile extension of an arterial street from United. The property is bordered by hayfields owned by acreage (non-farming) residents. U.S. Department of Agriculture census data inform that there were over 660 farms in the county in 1997. Across the road is a large milo field and drying bin, and the school board treasurer's cornfield lies kitty corner. North of the school, and up a hill for about one hundred yards, are railroad tracks that are in heavy use. The school building vibrates several times a day from long trains carrying coal from the Powder River Basin in Wyoming. The engineers always blow the horn when the students are outside of the school building.

When approaching the school from the east, a driver maneuvers under a viaduct, passes the board treasurer's farm and comes upon an unattractive, plain white, one-story building. This building is an old prefabricated school "portable" acquired in 1980 from a large school district in the Omaha area. The old Upper Rill School building was located in a semi-wetland, one mile west of the current site, and burned down after its chemical toilet caught fire. The school has two acres of field, enclosed by a four foot chain-link fence. There are makeshift kickball sites and a concrete basketball court, a four seat swing-set, a new jungle gym, and an antique county school merry-go-round that, as dangerous as it looks, gets plenty of use without injury.

State historical archives reveal that Upper Rill School district was formed in 1870 and retains almost its original geographic configuration. It takes its name from the small creek that flows through the district which is now only a trickle. The school district encompasses no population centers. The land in the district is composed of mostly family farms and some residential acreage property. The 1999 census indicates that there are 56 residents in the district, and 8 school age children, but only two are enrolled at Upper Rill. The rest "option out" or are home-schooled.

Students at Upper Rill This Year

In the 1999–2000 school year Upper Rill School has 10 students (see Table 3.3) serving four families. However, seven of these students do not reside in

Table 3.3.   Students at Upper Rill School, 1999–2000

Grade	Student
Pre–K	Danny
1st	Anna*†
2nd	Marlon
2nd	Mary*†
4th	Dylan
4th	Penny*†
5th	Nate*
6th	Scott*†
7h	Nora*†
8th	Danielle*†

* Those who reside in another district and are "option enrollment" students
† Erecksen siblings

the district and are "option enrollment" students. The parents of Big-hand's students reflects a diversity of occupational and educational backgrounds (see Table 3.4). The Erecksens' mother and father are college educated. None of these families considers itself poor, though certainly none consider themselves well off.

The Erecksen family resides in the Portage School district and options 6 children into Upper Rill. The Erecksens present an interesting twist on option enrollment in this particular setting. They are devout Missouri Synod Lutherans, a conservative, fundamentalist-leaning wing of the Lutheran Church. They have ten children total; the youngest is one year old and the oldest a high school junior (who attends classes though a local high home-school consortium). Until 1998, the mother, Nicole, home-schooled their children. While Nicole worked to coordinate with other home-school families in the area, the task of educating her children at home become overwhelming. Scott and Nicole were concerned that they could not properly attend to the education of all their children. Unlike most religious home-schooling families, the Erecksens reservations about public schools are not so much about curricular content (e.g., secular humanism or evolution), but about what the organization and culture of school would do to their children. Their religious values find fullest expression in the primacy of family unity. While the Erecksens are a "farm family" and carry values of shared obligation of upkeep of home and farm, unity of and attachment to the family are some predominant values. They tell that it is biblical. Nicole and Scott were concerned that public schooling, with its emphasis on graded classrooms, would separate their children from one

Table 3.4. Backgrounds of Upper Rill Students

	Parent Occupation		Parent Education (highest level achieved)	
Student	Mother	Father	Mother	Father
Erecksen Family Anna (K) Mary (2nd) Penny (4th) Robbie(6th) Nora (7th) Danielle (8th)	Stay at home. Part-time music teacher.	Farmer	Bachelor's Degree	Bachelor's Degree
Marlon (2nd) Danny (pre-K)	Registered Nurse	Welder, Truck Driver	Associate's Degree	Associate's Degree
Dylan (4th)	Office Manager for family business	Self-employed, demolition company	High School	High School
Nate (6th)	Hospital Technician	Stepfather: Warehouse Laborer Bio-father Real Estate Agent (out of state)	High School	Stepfather: High School Bio-Father: Unknown

another and erode the family structure. "We were concerned that the school would divide the kids, put pressure on them to be in cliques and not be brotherly or sisterly," as Scott put it to me. Scott and Nicole felt that the graded school system would impose division upon the children, urge them to become members of cliques, encourage resentment and sibling rivalry, and generally become accustomed to and value more highly a peer and popular culture than their family.

What was evident from the first few days that I got to know the Erecksen children at Upper Rill is that sense of obligation they have toward one another. They have near explicit family rules about deference of the younger children to older children and about the older children caring for the younger children. The children and their parents inform me that they instruct their children on sibling obligation, "to look out for another," to "help the younger ones if needed," and to make sure "everyone stays out of trouble." In my data collection and analysis I have always had a hard time imagining one Erecksen child in isolation from another. Scott and Nicole felt that the graded school system would impose division upon the children, become members of cliques, encourage resentment and sibling rivalry, and generally become accustomed to and value more highly a peer culture than their family.

Upper Rill effectively solved that problem for the Erecksens. The school allows them "to be together as much as possible next to home schooling," as Nicole puts it. And when they visited with the teacher the summer of 1998, before their children's enrollment, Scott indicates that they "kind of interviewed the teacher about his philosophy, and when he said that he wanted kids to think, we felt, 'How can you argue with that?'" The teacher, Will, informed them that there would be no room for religious instruction and they agreed. Both Nicole and Scott are college educated (the only Upper Rill parents who are) and Nicole has a teaching credential in music. In their informed judgment, Upper Rill was the next best thing to home schooling.

This was good news for Upper Rill which in 1998–1999 was facing another year of low enrollments. The school board had determined with their part-time contracted principal, Cal Booker, that they needed to average at least twelve students a year to roughly break even in per-pupil costs with the neighboring, affiliated Portage school district and to justify to the community staying open. As noted, that district's superintendent has stated repeatedly in public settings that he would like the school closed, primarily for property tax revenue that his district would absorb. The Erecksens immediately increased size of Upper Rill 150%.

Nate had been a student at Upper Rill since 2nd grade. He originally lived in the district until 1997, when his mother remarried and moved to United. He is now an option student and makes the fifteen minute car commute to the school. Nate is also the only student to receive special education services though a traveling special education teacher and speech pathologist who both come twice a week for one hour.

Dylan is new this year. His parents purchased property in the school district and have built a new house. They previously resided in Dark Glen, the small town immediately to the west of the schools. His parents indicate that they were happy for the transfer of schools since Dylan was identified as a potential special education student and was having behavior problems at Dark Glen Elementary School. They have become very satisfied with Upper Rill and the teacher.

The only children that reside in the district are Marlon and his brother Danny. Both their mother and father attended Upper Rill. Their grandfather also attended the school and is currently the treasurer (and unquestionable power broker) of the school board. Danny is not a formally enrolled student. He turned 5 in January, and thus missed the October birthday cut-off for kindergarten eligibility in Nebraska. He did not attend the school the first semester. Danny had been attending pre-school in United, where his mother works as a nurse. She asked the teacher if Danny could attend the school when he turned five as a "semi-kindergartner," with the idea that he would attend kindergarten full-time the following year. This was both matter of convenience and education for the Schmidts. The sheer proximity of the school made Danny's custodial care easier. Like the Erecksens, the Schmidts felt it important that Danny be with his older brother. Additionally, they felt that he could get a "head start" at kindergarten, making "real kindergarten" an easy transition. The teacher agreed, and decided with the parents that he would do some "basic stuff" with Danny such as writing his letters and numbers, letting him sit in on oral readings with the first and second graders, and have him read some age appropriate books with older children.

Another Rural and Intimate School

Like Bighand School, Upper Rill School has a combination of ruralness and intimacy. In addition to being "in the country," in an agricultural community, and historically the school for the area's farm children, all the currently enrolled children have connection to agriculture presently or in their recent family histories. The Erecksen family is the only Upper Rill family that farms for a living and their children make up over half the students. Marlon and Danny's mother and father grew up farming. Marlon's father still helps out his father, a full-time farmer (and the school board treasurer) with harvest. Marlon says one of his favorite things to do is to ride in the combine with his grandfather during harvest. Until Nate moved to United after his mother's remarriage, he lived in his mother's family farmhouse.

And like Bighand School intimacy accompanies this ruralness at Upper Rill, making it an intimately rural place. The intimacy derives from at least three sources. For one, the Erecksen children bring what is to an outsider like me a palpable emotional attachment to one another. They spend nearly their entire waking hours around each other and this is extended at school. The more immersed I became in the life of the school, the harder it became for me to imagine an Erecksen child in isolation from another. This family tightness and their collective presence has not created a boundary between them and the other students; they are not considered an "odd" family by the teacher, school board members or others with whom I have spoken in the community. In other words their family tightness has not seemed to create a family boundary at the school, making an "Erecksen clique" or some community kind of oddity.

Second, Upper Rill is the only school that Marlon has ever attended and Nate since first grade. These two boys have known each other and interacted closely *in school* for four years. Two years prior there were only three students at Upper Rill, and Marlon and Nate were two of them. It is hard for either of them to think of their schooling without thinking about each other and the one full-time teacher they have had (see below). The teacher considers Nate the most "senior" of the students at the school. Nate, Marlon and their teacher have created for each other the chief source of sustained school relationships.

Lastly, because of the small number of students, school relationships are shaped through the students' and teacher's daily co-inhabitance of a rather small space for over eight months of the year. They are simply regular parts of each other's lives. As I indicate in Chapter 5, they cannot avoid each other in either their academic interactions nor their non-academic interactions. They play, eat and do academic work together. It is through this mundane interaction they become familiar with each other. Like Bighand School, this is an intimacy that comes from knowing, and being known by, others.

"Teacher Will"

The teacher, Will Tomlinson, is in his fifth year at Upper Rill. The students affectionately refer to him as "Teacher Will." It is not uncommon to hear students (and parents) call him "Will," or sometimes just "Teacher." His three syllable surname, along with the title "mister," make it cumbersome for the students to pronounce. As Nora says of the name Teacher Will, "It's just easier to say. He doesn't mind." Marlon implies it is a term of endearment, "It shows we like him. He doesn't care that we use his first name."

Will came to teaching after an 18 year career as a railroad brakeman. He started college after high school but dropped out after a semester. He returned to college in 1993 at a vocationally oriented liberal arts college. Will says he pursued teaching because it is something that he says he always wanted to do. He notes the intense boredom, danger, and physical burden of railroad work that led him to pursue a second career. Before coming to Upper Rill, he spent a year teaching kindergarten in another Class One, two-teacher school in the same county and with the same principal. When the opening at Upper Rill become available Will immediately applied for and acquired the job. His only professional teaching jobs have been in small country schools.

The country school was new for Will when he started teaching. He grew up in United and attended large, graded elementary schools. His teacher education was oriented toward graded elementary schools. All his practical experiences in his teacher education program were in larger schools. He still lives in United with his family and grown children. Will at first blush appears an oddly gruff character. His avocation is martial arts and frequently refers to it as a source of educational edification (e.g,. self-discipline, hard work, courtesy and respect). That he is male makes him a peculiarity in the world of Class One and one-teacher schools in Nebraska, not to mention elementary school teaching in general. Tall and middle-aged, he wears Birkenstock sandals and, when it is warm, Hawaiian shirts and shorts (I always thought he looked like he was on vacation, especially when he plays kickball with the students for "gym class"). Culturally and educationally speaking, Will's experience is removed from the rural Nebraska, the Upper Rill community and one-room schooling. As he says tersely, "There is nothing rural about me."

The students uniformly report a strong affection for Will. While they describe him as quietly demanding (like a martial arts "sensei" or master), they see him as good-natured (all use the word "nice"). Nate laughs when he tells that Teacher Will "does not stand for bull...oney." And, these students say that Will truly believes in the two signs posted in the school. One adorning his bulletin board, directly behind his chair and slightly above his head, has the encircled word CAN'T with diagonal line running through it. On the opposite wall is a twelve by eighteen inch placard that reads THINK in Cyrillic-looking letters.

One Thursday during my observations early in the school year, Will was visibly frustrated with Dylan's lack of effort to complete a social studies assignment. Dylan repeatedly claimed to Will that he could not complete the exercise (answering one of those questions found at the end of the chapter about a passage in that chapter). "I can't," he stated audibly at least twice. It is worth noting that Dylan's transition to Upper Rill had not been completely smooth. Will told me that he was convinced that Dylan had "learned how to give up" at his previous school (in neighboring Dark Glen) and that his teachers accepted his excuses, letting Dylan conclude that "he was the fat kid who couldn't learn." In other words, deep down, Will claims, the teachers at Dark Glen did not care about, or at least did not care to understand, Dylan and relegated him to "low achieving" status and put him "on the fast track to special ed." In other words, Will interpreted in and around Dylan a self-fulfilling prophecy. He says he felt that Dylan had acquired a habit of manipulating his teachers into feeling sorry for him, lowering their expectations, ultimately letting him get out of doing his academic work, and that Dylan was effectively "set up to fail."

Will went over the social studies question with Dylan several times, and Will said that it is straightforward as to be something that "second graders could do." Will asked Dylan, "Are you jerking my chain?" He then said to Dylan, from his desk and in full hearing range of all students, "Dylan. Listen to me. Helplessness is a learned behavior. I want you to think about that today as much as you can." Will gently repeated "Helplessness is a learned behavior" four more times to Dylan, who he nodded his head affirmatively. When I asked him later what he thought that meant, Dylan shrugged his shoulders and mumbled something that sounded like, "I dunno."

To an outsider visiting this school, this interaction between Will and Dylan might appear coarse: a teacher berating a 10 year old boy in one of those unintended power struggles that teachers neither intend or enjoy. But this reveals a deeper aspect of the school, the sense of attachment and obligation the teacher and students have toward one another, specifically the rights and role of the teacher at the school. This reflects part of the students' shared understanding—an unstated social contract—that Will has a right to push students because he cares about them and, in the end, is "nice." This is induced in no small measure by the small setting, where the teacher and students are present to each other almost continually. Consequently, in Nate's words, "There's no place to hide; Will knows what your doing *constantly*" (emphasis his). Dylan emphatically says there is "not, no way I'm going back to D-Glen [Elementary school]. *They're mean!*" He went on to say that "Teacher Will cares about me, even though he gives me [a] hard time sometimes. He knows I was jerking his chain."

This vignette of Dylan and Will points to the far-reaching control Will has established at the school and the students' assent to this control. This plays into Will's teaching in a significant way, as I describe in Chapter 5.

NOTES

1. Data on Nebraska Schools come from the Nebraska State Department of Education Data Center and from the rural education advocacy Group Class Ones United.

2. Some state senator (typically from one of the "metropolitan" areas of Omaha and Lincoln) predictably puts forward a bill that makes consolidation a central feature of school financing.

3. The other official school Classes are A, B, C-1, C-2, D-1, D-2. These are ranked in order of size, with Class A being the largest and D-2 the smallest. There is also "Class Six" districts that are high school only and are often the consolidated high school for a constellation of several Class Ones.

4. I visited in 1997 a Class One school that had 2 students. Upper Rill School had 3 students in 1996.

5. Descendents of the original Bighand family still own farm property in the district. I discovered that the name Bighand is the Anglo transliteration of the German "Grossehand." This name is a pseudonym. However, the teacher and her administrators refer to the school by its district number, which I omit here for confidentiality reasons. There is also mistaken lore in the community that "Bighand" was the name of an Indian tribe that at one time inhabited the area. There has never been a tribe of "Bighand" Indians in North America.

6. There are nine other eligible students in the district. They attend either a private school in Riverview City, are home schooled, or "optioned" into a neighboring Class One district. One of these nine is Daisy's brother Tom, a 7th grader at Riverview Middle School. His mother transferred him last year

from Bighand partly because she said he was restless, "unchallenged" and because he was the only boy his age at a school with five older girls.
7.   I am deliberately omitting population sizes of these communities since to indicate these would provide data making them readily identifiable.

REFERENCES

DeWalt, M. (1997). *One-room school: Current trend in public and private education*. Winthrop University.

Leight, R. L., & Rhienhart, A. D. (1992). Revisiting Americana: One-room school in retrospect. *The Educational Forum, 56*(2), 135–151.

Lerner, A.J., & Loewe, F. (1959). *My Fair Lady* (1956 original Broadway cast recording). New York: Columbia Records.

Muse I, Hite, S., Randall, V., & Jensen, A. (1998). One-teacher schools in America. *Teacher Educator, 33*(3), 141–149.

Peshkin, A. (1974/1994). *Growing up American: Schooling and the survival of community*. Waveland Press.

CHAPTER 4

GETTING THROUGH

Academic Life at Bighand School

This chapter describes the culture and practices of Bighand School and how being educated and "doing school" are defined there. My specific concern is the organization of instruction. Though the teacher feels that her twelve students are too numerous this year (too many different children and too many subjects), the school's size plays into her creation of an effective vehicle for a particular form of instruction geared toward getting students through generic standardized curricula. Daily instruction at Bighand is carried out entirely in grade-level recitations. While these occur other children quietly attend to their individual bookwork for their own recitations. In recitations, the teacher directs and supervises academic work, which consists entirely of discrete workbook and textbook assignments. The teacher is controller and disseminator of knowledge via textbooks in these recitations. These recitations resemble the form of the old country school recitation described by educational historians, but with a modified focus on written assignments not oral performance. Successful schooling is defined as the students' demonstrated progress through these commercially produced materials and accompanying exams in order to keep up with town school counterparts and to be ready for middle or secondary school. The school's modern recitation-based pedagogy is highly refined

Naturally Small: Teaching and Learning in the Last of the One-Room Schools, pages 33–57
Copyright © 2004 by Information Age Publishing
All rights of reproduction in any form reserved.

and extraordinarily functional when viewed in light of the local definitions of schooling and school success.

DEFINING A PEDAGOGICAL PROBLEM: KEEPING UP AND BEING READY

Mrs. Hoffman faces a classic problem of the country school teacher: How to organize academic work for twelve different children, at six different grade levels, across multiple subject areas that is acceptable to the school board, parents, administrative authorities, community members (who are often graduates of one-teacher schools and Bighand School) and her own sense of a proper education? Early in the school year I asked her what she sees as the major task she faces. She responded succinctly:

> I've got a lot of kids this year. Too many kids, in a lot of grades, if you ask me. Some people will say, "You only have 12 kids this year. What are you complaining about?" Well, you teach all these kids all their subjects and tell me how easy it is! But this is the way things are in one-room schools. [exasperated laughter] They've always been this way. Sometimes you have a few kids and sometimes you have a lot all in the same grade. Other years you get 'em spread out like this. This is about as bad as I've had it, I think...It's tough and it wears you down; there's so much to do and so much to keep track of. But parents have got to know about their kids' progress...and kids have to be ready for middle school or high school. They can't get anything that's too weird.

Mrs. Hoffman defines this problem in terms of ensuring students complete an identifiable grade-level curricular program. In the absence of a graded classroom and a graded school culture around her, Mrs. Hoffman sees that her primary tasks are to make sure that individual students are demonstratively "at grade level" and that they are "keeping up with," and possibly exceeding, students in a large graded elementary or middle schools in, for instance, Sparta or Riverview. She is further concerned that the students not become immersed in an alien curriculum—"anything that's too weird"—but in one that feeds into, or is compatible with, what the students will encounter in secondary school and for some who transfer early to middle school (such as Daisy and Kimberly who will both transfer next year to Riverview Middle School). As she sees it, her pedagogical task is to organize academic work for individual students to "get through" in order to demonstrate that they are at grade level and be ready for transfer to middle or secondary school. It is, to her, just common sense. While on the surface this seems like a generalized concern for any teacher in any school, this defined educational problem, and practices that flow from it, take on a particular hue in this one-teacher school.

A Problem of Common Sense

To Mrs. Hoffman, her concerns are just common sense and, therefore, require little explaining or articulation. As such, they are deeply embedded in the culture and history of one-teacher schooling, in community expectations and in Mrs. Hoffman's own experiences as a student and as a teacher. As Clifford Geertz (1983) has pointed out, "common sense" comprises its own cultural system and is, therefore, generally tacit, not an overly conscious set of organized propositions. It is composed of implicitly held beliefs that are, to the insiders, self-evident as to their goodness, value and truth. Questioning common sense means questioning its immutability and prestige. Mrs. Hoffman says this problem she faces is simply a matter of "the way things are in our one-room schools," and that "[t]hey've always been this way." This is not a statement of ignorance. Taken from a more culturally sensitive point of view, it represents a conventional response embedded in the widely distributed view of what a *country* school like Big-hand is presently for: ensuring kids are ready for secondary school and keeping up with vaguely identified students in "town schools."

Parent and Administrator Expectations

Mrs. Hoffman's common sense approach is comfortably situated within the more obvious expectations of her administrators and parents. While the administrators and parents indicate other, more nuanced goals and values of a one-teacher school, notably the benefit of a kind of surveillance and scrutiny and a measure of community control afforded by the small setting (I focus on these values as context for instruction in the next chapter), they all explicitly indicate the importance of students "keeping up" with other kids at other schools and "being ready" for middle or secondary school. Parents indicate that they expect the school to effectively offer their children a competitive academic advantage. As Molly's mother puts it, "They learn things here that they don't in town schools," such as "doing their work well." All these families could readily "option" their children to at least one of the surrounding school districts and conceivably to one of the nearby Class Ones. Their responses seem almost rehearsed when I ask them what they see as the academic mission of the school: that kids are ready to move on. The words of Tom, Mary, and Susan's father echo that of other parents:

> I'm not saying that the kids can't get an education in Sparta or Riverview [elementary and middle schools]. It's just that this is our local school and we think the teacher can do just as good, if not better, job of preparing the stu-

dents for high school classes. Other things go with this [schooling at Big-hand] that is important. But our Jana has not had many academic problems, and we hope that for the other two as well...She [Mrs. Hoffman] does have to be on top of things, otherwise our kids start high school at a disadvantage. That would not be acceptable...I would say most people feel that way around here.

Tom is correct, most parents do say they feel this way. These parental expectations feed into and support a widely held view as to the purpose of schooling at Bighand and, moreover, the authority of the administrators to grant its legitimacy. The majority of the parents I spoke with automatically defer to the principal and county superintendent's expertise and assume that they are doing what is best for the school and, by extension, their kids. Parental support for the administrators is not, however, universal. Kimberly and David's parents question whether they really know what Mrs. Hoffman is doing and how she interacts with students in the course of an average school day (connected to their general discontent with Mrs. Hoffman). But they recognize that they are a minority and that Mrs. Hoffman has already survived an insurrection in the late 1980s.[1] So they feel they cannot challenge administrative authority.

Both the relevant administrators of Bighand School are long-standing members of the county and recognized as well-traveled school administrators. The principal, Jim Hauser, is a retired principal from Sparta Schools, and the county superintendent,[2] Stan Vogt, is a retired superintendent of a rural district in an adjacent county. Their longevity extends to them a strong measure of respect and authority. Consequently, these administrators carry with them not only a sanctioned authority in matters of curriculum, in their official service to the school board, but also a generally recognized local cultural authority within the community. They both stress the need to confidently tell parents and people in the community, whether at public events such as school board meetings or privately, that the students are "up to speed" and that their school's state accreditation is not in jeopardy. Thus Jim Hauser indicates that kids keeping up and "being ready to transfer" is "what has to happen in these schools if the country kids are to compete and survive" in secondary school. And Stan Vogt speaks of the need of these schools "to have strong relations with the affiliated [high] schools, and the best way to do that is be sure that the kids are prepared to go to high school."

Generally speaking the parents, community members, administrators and the teacher are implicitly, as Tom says, "on the same page" as to what the school is about. Broadly defined in this community, *keeping up* and *being ready* is what schooling at Bighand is for. Mrs. Hoffman is not merely carrying out dictates from her administrative superiors; she is steeped in these expectations, personally and professionally. She is taking part in the larger socially constructed idea that school for *all* Bighand students is for keeping up with "town school" kids and being ready for their inevitable enrollment in one of three high schools, and some students' enrollment to the middle school in Riverview or to the K–8 school in Sparta. This fashions and reinforces Mrs. Hoffman's common sense definition of her pedagogical problem. While ultimately a simple and straightforward view of the problem, this nevertheless profoundly shapes Mrs. Hoffman's view of her role in daily school practices and leads her to create a highly refined system of instruction.

GETTING THROUGH TEXTBOOKS AND WORKBOOKS

To address this defined teaching problem, Mrs. Hoffman organizes with and for a modified, academic standardization. She states emphatically her belief in "a strict adherence to a fixed curriculum." What is her fixed curriculum? There is no Nebraska, county, country school or "Class One" curriculum. Nor is there a curriculum required from any one of three affiliated K–12 districts. Bighand's curriculum is organized exclusively around commercially produced textbook and workbook series that are grade specific. Textbooks and workbooks *are* the curriculum at Bighand School. Mrs. Hoffman uses only those produced by major textbook publishing companies. She does not limit herself to one company or series. These include Houghton-Mifflin, Scott/Foresman & Co., Silver Burdett & Ginn, Holt, Rinehart, & Winston, Saxon Math, all textbook industry names familiar to teachers. When she says 2nd grade reading, this means Houghton-Mifflin's grade 2 reading series (this year's included the basal *Spinners* [1987]). While she communicates occasionally with other Class One school teachers, and is informed by the school's contracted administrator and the county superintendent of the textbooks that neighboring school districts use, Mrs. Hoffman does not strictly follow these in her choices for textbook and workbook series. She uses these "to get an idea" of what other schools are using. Sometimes textbooks are recommendations from the Educational Service Unit.[3] Sometimes Mrs. Hoffman inquires into the local affiliated school districts as to their textbooks. She even obtained several series from an auction at another country school that had closed down.

Mrs. Hoffman puts a great deal of faith in these texts for her curricular organization. The specific content of the textbooks is not a major concern for her. Nor does she express any preference for a specific series, hence listing them all is practically irrelevant. Mrs. Hoffman's criteria for these textbook and workbook series are not explicit, at least as she talked with me about them. Plainly put, textbooks and workbooks have for her face-validity and represent reliably the grade levels they are designed for because major textbook producers are established companies and the books are in widespread use.

Importantly, the county superintendent and the principal similarly presume the dominant place of these textbooks as curriculum organizers and they support and approve of Mrs. Hoffman's usage of the them. Both agree on the importance of using "curriculum materials" comparable to those in surrounding school districts. The principal speaks vaguely of a need for "uniformity" and the county superintendent about "compatibility" with these districts. Yet neither can specify the content of that uniformity and compatibility when pressed. With the teacher, they just assume that these textbook and workbook series are compatible and inhere some uniformity because of their generic features. A 5th grade basal reader is a 5th grade basal reader, whether published by companies such as Holt or Silver-Burdett. The administrators state that their concerns are for the books to be current, and this itself is not clear as to its criteria since some textbooks are more 10 ten years old.[4]

I call this a modified standardization in that it is not a matter of Mrs. Hoffman aligning rigidly her curriculum with any one or all or the other Class One schools in the county. Nor does she align hers with Sparta, Riverview or Surrey K–12 school districts. I made a few phone calls and found out that each of these school districts uses different and often multiple textbooks and workbooks. For her to specifically align or standardize with one district's textbooks would invite conflict with the parents whose children will attend one of the other two affiliated districts. It is hard to see any of the compatibility or uniformity, except in the very broadest of senses (i.e., that they are all graded series). The standardization at Bighand comes in the use of grade-level textbooks and workbooks alone.

Textbooks are intended for mass distribution and meant to serve as many school districts as possible (sales volume is obviously important for these companies). Generic in form and content, they are directed at an average student and an average school district curriculum. Textbooks are sometimes revised according to particular states' needs, such as California's in mathematics (see Wilson, 2003), according to national standards, e.g., National Science Foundation funded Reform Curriculum (see Senk & Thompson, 2002), because the markets are so large and amenable. By definition, textbooks are designed for as many students, schools and districts as possible and none in particular. I suspect that individual textbook companies, and not a few school district curriculum coordinators, might heartily disagree. But how textbooks are designed and how teachers construe *and* use them are very different things.[5] In many ways, textbooks represent a *de facto* national curriculum (see Kliebard [1986] on the historical and central role of textbooks in a standardized, de facto national curriculum).

Subsequently, Mrs. Hoffman's "strict adherence" to any one of the text-book series she acquires is in effect a strict adherence to the fixed curriculum offered by any textbook series published by a major, national textbook company. Because these textbooks and workbooks are, for the most part, directed at a generalized and *de facto* national curriculum, their use is the way that Mrs. Hoffman and the administrators can claim (and demonstrate) to the school's constituents that they are concerned with students acquiring a portable and versatile education. This, in turn, will prepare students for *any* secondary school and offers an implicit comparison of Bighand School's student progress to that of town schools. More significantly, it is what Mrs. Hoffman does with the textbooks that render their specific features nearly immaterial.

This place of textbooks is not a recent trait of Midwestern country schooling. Since their inception in the Midwest in nineteenth century, country schools have traditionally relied heavily on textbooks (see Theobald, 1995). Since these schools were at first staffed by young women, often just out of secondary school with little or no higher education and minimal (by today's standards) formal teacher education, textbooks assumed a place of great importance. Local school boards and county and state authorities could not rely on teachers to have the knowledge to teach all subjects. Teachers were not trusted to be knowledgeable enough to teach the subjects and were required to use textbooks as strict instructional frameworks. Recall that Mrs. Hoffman started teaching at age 18, with a provisional teaching certificate in a country school. Thus this centrality of textbooks at Bighand can be attributed, in part, to the historical residue of their significance within country schooling. It may also carry with it a concealed distrust of the teacher. But, more immediately and reliably, their use represents a conventional and functional response to Mrs. Hoffman's need to *get through* as defined by the problem of *keeping up* and *being ready*. Their use makes unqualified sense, in this setting.

ORGANIZATION OF CURRICULUM
AND TEACHING FOR GETTING THROUGH

The usage of textbooks and the value of "a strict adherence to a fixed curriculum," are, of course, not limited to country schools. It is surely not difficult to locate a teacher or school that uses textbooks in this way, especially in an age of standards-based reforms and high stakes accountability. How textbooks are used and implicated in Mrs. Hoffman's teaching practice, as a way of coping with her defined instructional challenge is, however, particular to this one-teacher school circumstance: to get 12 children through a standardized curriculum. This school is not, for instance, composed of all

2nd or 6th graders who ostensibly go through the same subject matter at about the same time, as might be found in a large and graded school. Rather, there are 6 different grade levels, and up to three individuals in each of those, not to mention the individual variation within those grade levels. In teacher parlance, excluding kindergarten, she has to keep her mind focused on at least five "preparations" for each subject. When I ask her what the school curriculum is, she points to the textbooks. Textbooks offer Mrs. Hoffman a way to cope with this challenge of organizing her work to get students through a curriculum and to demonstrate their keeping up and readiness for transfer to middle or secondary school.

Classes

In Bighand school there is no whole class instruction in any subjects. There are no group projects within or across grade levels.[6] Instruction is carried out entirely in what are locally called "classes." Classes are grade level specific. When I began my observations at the beginning of the school year—the first day of school—I was struck by the almost frenetic pace at which the students cycle through these classes. A class involves small groups of students of the same grade level, or individual students, sitting at the teacher's table for short periods of interaction, rarely more than fifteen minutes. It is the shared understanding among the Mrs. Hoffman and the students that these classes are designed as routinized opportunities for the teacher to: check student work; briefly introduce a new subject topic, which is invariably the next chapter, lesson or unit within a student's or students' textbook; return to students their corrected and recorded assignments, quizzes or tests, if they have not been returned already; direct students to the next assignment, invariably connected to an ensuing chapter, lesson or unit; listen to students read aloud (excerpts from textbook passages or assignment directions); and record and keep track of student advancement through the assignments. While these short classes take place, those students who are not "in class" are expected to follow the generalized rule, unless authorized by the teacher, to work independently and very quietly on their assignments and readings at their desks, sometimes at the computer (as a reward for completing all assignments, leaving them with extra time) or with the teacher's aide. At one point, I counted a dizzying 28 classes in one day. Mrs. Hoffman reports to the school board that she has had 30 in one day. From my data, the average number hovers around 23. That she perceives herself as taking on up to 30 classes daily indicates her sense of their pervasiveness in her school life.

Classes follow a set schedule. This schedule is posted as the "Daily Program" in the front of the room (see Table 4.1). According to the county superintendent, law in Class One schools requires the prominent display of

Table 4.1. The "Daily Program" Posted in the Front of the Schoolroom

Begins	Time	Grade	Recitations In	Tue–Thurs (Kindergarten)
			Morning	
8:30	10 min	All	Opening	
8:40	35 min	1st–6th	Reading	Reading Readiness
9:15	15 min	8th	Literature	Free time
9:30	30 min	1–8	Spelling (Tests-Friday)	Math
10:00	15 min	All	Recess	
10:17	20 min	1–6th	Phonics (Ind. Work)	Phonics
10:20	55 min	1–8th	English	Quiet Activity
11:00	15 min	1–8th	Writing-Journals	Computer
	30 min	K–2	Computer	Individual Time
11:15	15 min			Storytime
11:25		All	Wash hands	
11:30	30 min	All	Lunch	
			Afternoon	
12:00	15 min	1–2	Reading	Rest
12:00	15 min	5–8	Free Reading	
12:15	40 min	1–2	Math	
12:55	50 min	5–8	Math (Tue-Wed Test)	Free Quiet Activity
		5–8	Computer Time	
1:45	10 min	All	Recess-P.E.	
2:00	55 min	1st	Health	Science
2:00		8th	Science (Mon and Wed)	
			Science Experiments	
2:00	55 min	All	Social Studies Tue-Thurs (workbooks)	Map Skills
2:00	55 min	1–8th	Art-Friday	Kindergarten: Art (Thursday)
2:55	5 min	All	Jobs	
3:00		All	Dismiss	

the poster. This schedule is modified only slightly and infrequently, usually around field trips and special events such as preparation for the Christmas and Spring "programs."

What intrigued me about these "classes" is that they echoed old country school "recitations" described by educational historians (e.g., Cuban, 1994; Theobald, 1995). What triggered this connection for me was the heading *Recitations In,* where conceivably the term "subject" might be, that led me to consider whether this onslaught of "classes" is a version of the old country school recitation manifest in a modern one-teacher school. The organization of instruction yields some parallels to these old recitations that I address later in this chapter.

Organization of Classes

In Bighand School the organization of instruction is the organization of classes. A class is a straightforward event. While the students sit in uneven rows facing the blackboard, what is considered the front of the room (see Figure 4.1 for the map of the room), Mrs. Hoffman sits in the center of a U-shaped table at the left hand corner of the front, facing the students. Her table acts as her desk, with teaching materials, grade and plan books, and small piles of student work. More significantly, from the students' point of view, it is where classes take place. While she can oversee the entire school from her desk, she is typically preoccupied with classes and record keeping. She relies on students to "discipline themselves" and each other

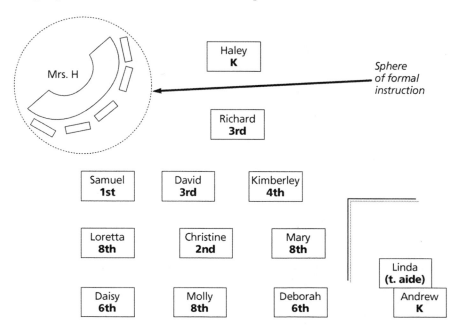

Figure 4.1.   Classroom seating arrangement, top floor at Bighand school.

through adherence to long-standing and unwritten rules about "no talk-ing" to each other outside of classes, "no more than two people [walking] on the floor at one time," and requesting permission to go to the toilet, the library (bookcases in the back of the room), the computer, or to another student for help. These rules, she tells, help students concentrate on their work and is ready for their classes.

During classes, Mrs. Hoffman is in closer proximity to and direct inter-action with students around their academic work. She is central to the interaction, directing students through their assignments, having them show her that they have done their assigned work, and occasionally check-ing for (what is for her) evidence of student learning, or what she says is "getting what they are supposed to." They share the understanding that the teacher's table is a special place for a specific kind of interaction.

There is a generalized pattern to the classes that cuts across subjects or the "Recitations In." Mrs. Hoffman usually calls students of a particular grade to class and the students sit in the chairs facing her. It is not uncom-mon for her to announce the order of classes in a given stretch of time. Sometimes students will individually approach the table with their materi-als anticipating their class and stand quietly waiting for her to authorize them to sit down. Once seated at the table, Mrs. Hoffman usually returns the previous day's assignment, quiz or test from a standardized textbook/ workbook series. She has graded these papers and students immediately look for their scores on the assignment or test. Mrs. Hoffman has an implied minimal standard of around 85% correct for passing these assign-ments, quizzes or tests (e.g., no less than 17 correct math problems out of 20). As she returns these, she nearly always points out the missed questions or problems. However, Mrs. Hoffman rarely tells students "in class" of the inadequacy of their work. She usually tells them well before class, either calling the student up to her table or walking over to him/her. She informs the student quietly, yet still very publicly in front of the entire school, in order to give the student the chance to correctly complete it and return it to her. Otherwise, this opening sequence of the class involves mild praise for students for successful completion of work.

Mrs. Hoffman views this opening sequence as simply making sure stu-dents is ready for class, i.e., that her "class time" is used efficiently. How-ever, she does this making sure well before the students come to class. This authority praise built into this sequence is not lost on the students. As Molly, one of the veteran 8th graders, puts it: "She tells us we're doing OK. How else could she have class if we didn't finish [assignments, tests] OK?" When I asked her if this makes her feel good when she is told that she is "doing OK", Molly looked at me out of the sides of her eyes, cracked a half smile and said with an economy of words characteristic of people in her community, "Pretty much." It can be inferred, then, that in this indirect praising Mrs. Hoffman reinforces her evaluative authority over the students in a close, face to face setting, and one in which the students generally feel positive. Classes, for the Bighand student, almost always get off to a gratifying start.

After this opening sequence, Mrs. Hoffman declares that it is time to proceed to the next chapter, unit, or lesson in the textbook at hand. This sequence involves Mrs. Hoffman directing a student to read aloud the introduction of a new lesson, unit or chapter. In the case of reading, the first classes in the morning, she directs students to the next story in the basal reader. She will ask a student to start the story, and she has them read aloud, in round-robin fashion with students alternating paragraphs or pages, until she determines their time is up. She directs students to complete the reading and points out "Comprehension Questions" at the end of the basal story chapter they are to answer in writing.

In other subjects, like math, Mrs. Hoffman directs a student to read the directions for the textbook/workbook assignment, and then asks that student or another to read aloud through the "example, or "sample" problem(s) or exercise(s). Mrs. Hoffman then directs them to complete the assignment for the following day's class. For social studies, this involves something of a combination of turn taking reading aloud and going over questions or directions for assignments. Classes end as Mrs. Hoffman writes down in her plan book the lesson or chapter that is to be completed, or story to be read, and the assignment or exercise to be completed.

INSTANCES OF READING AND MATH CLASSES

In order to render a greater sense of what this kind of instruction is like, I present excerpts from two classes, second grade reading and fifth grade math. These classes took place the same day, February 17, 1999. I selected these particular classes for the simple reason that they are mundane, utterly representative of classes as a whole at Bighand. They are both short, highly focused academic activities in the middle of the school year. And they are among the only classes that Mrs. Hoffman permitted me to audio-tape record.[7] These two live action instances of classes highlight the general pattern of instruction. In each we see Mrs. Hoffman not only managing the textbook-base curriculum but also, as in the case of 2nd grade reading, how she manages students and the quiet flow of activity around her. There are twenty five classes on this day. The second grade reading class takes place early in the school day at 8:49 AM and the fifth grade math class takes place at 1:15 PM (see Table 4.2).

Table 4.2.   "Classes" for Wednesday, February 17, 1999

Time	Duration (Minutes)	Subject	Grade/Student
8:36 AM	3	Reading	1st grade—Samuel
8:40	7	Reading	2nd grade—Richard
8:49	9	Reading	2nd grade—David, Christine
8:59	10	Reading	6th grade
9:10	16	Reading	8th grade
9:37	22	Spelling	2nd grade
10:45	2	English	6th grade
10:47	6	English	1st grade
10:54	5	English	6th grade
11:05	7	English	8th grade
12:05 PM	4	Reading	1st grade
12:10	9	Reading	2nd grade—David, Christine
12:21	8	Reading	2nd grade—Richard alone
12:35	7	Reading	2nd grade—David, Christine cont'd
12:47	7	Math	2nd grade
1:01	6	Math	8th grade
1:15	5	Math	5th grade
1:21	2	Math	6th grade
1:25	4	Math	1st grade
1:35	10	Social Studies	2nd grade
2:00	8	Social Studies	6th grade
2:15	7	Social studies	1st grade
2:24	12	Science	8th grade
2:38	8	Science	6th grade
2:48	5	Science	5th grade

A 2nd Grade Reading Class

This second grade reading class involves David and Christine specifically. Although Richard is seated at the table, he is not part of the class directly. Immediately prior to this, he was in a "reading class" by himself with Mrs. Hoffman. At this point in the school year, Mrs. Hoffman continues to have great difficulty in disciplining Richard. Both she and the other students speak of him not having learned to be a student at Bighand and continuing to present a challenge to the culture of the school. That is, he has had a rough period of socialization into the everyday routine of Bighand School. This day Mrs. Hoffman is having him sit next to her so as to monitor his work and discipline him if necessary without shouting across the room. She has decided that even though he may continue to be disruptive, she can better handle him if he is near her. This is somewhat awkward for Richard since he is a 2nd grader along with Christine and David. He told me bluntly and clearly that he does not like being singled out like this and that this happened a lot at the school he attended the previous year. Mrs. Hoffman has him reading in a different textbook that is actually ahead of Christine and David's. Consequently, in this strip of activity, Richard is seated to Mrs. Hoffman's left, but is not taking turns reading pages in the story and we see Mrs. Hoffman imploring him to read his own book. It is as if he is put in the position of observer rather than participant, though we do see him try to involve himself.

Mrs. Hoffman has returned to Christine and David their written answers to the comprehension questions from the last story. The day before they were informed of the story, "The Picture" (Marshall, 1989), and came prepared to read it aloud. Mrs. Hoffman does not indicate to Christine where she should begin only that she should begin. Later I found out that Mrs. Hoffman had not read the story herself, though she said she remembers it from the having taught it a few years ago. Christine and David take turns reading pages of the story while Richard looks on and interjects comments.

2nd Grade Reading Interaction

The following transcript represents approximately seven minutes of a complete reading class. Words in italics represent a verbatim oral reading of the text. The utterances that are indented occur while another is talking, as in overlapping speech.

Mrs. Hoffman: Let's get to your story.
    Richard: Tah dah. [opening his on reading book, announcing to Mrs. Hoffman that he is ready to do his own work].
Mrs. Hoffman: Christine go ahead and start.
    Christine: *One day rabbit came to the beach. "Wow," he said, I must paint a picture of the beach."*
    MH: Did he like the beach?
Christine: Yes.
    MH: He thought it was beautiful. What do you think this is? [addressing Christine, pointing to the picture in the textbook]
    Richard: That's a weird beach. [Mrs. Hoffman does not respond]
Christine: Mmm. [shrugs shoulders]

MH: Where do they grow palm tress?

Richard: Cocoa nuts.

MH: And where would they, where would you go to see palm trees?

David: The beach!

MH: What country would you go to? Or what state would you go to?

David: Virginia Beach.

MH: Might be. Why don't they, how about Hawaii?

Richard: Hawaii, yea!

MH: That would be nice, wouldn't it.

Sarah: [from her desk] Ah-hem. Christine your feet. [tells her to not tap her feet]

MH: Yeah, well.

Christine: [resumes reading] *So he sat down. Soon he painted the sky and water.*

Richard: That looks weird, green water.

MH: This is kind of over here green too [pointing to the sky].

Christine: [resumes] *"This is a lot of fun" he said. "I really liked my picture."*

MH: Richard get your reading book out.

Richard: [mumbles] Alright.

Christine: *Just then a dog walked by. "Oh no" said the dog. "That's not –That's not right the sky is too blow –blue. "Put in more white."*

MH: Alright. Look how dark it is. If you add some white to it's going to get lighter. It will look more like that [points to the page].

Richard: Cause if it is dark it will look like it's winter.

MH: Mmm. It will look like a storm coming. Okay here you are [pointing to Richard's page, reminding him that he is supposed to be reading a different story in a different book].

David: *"No thank you," said the rabbit. "I like it my way. Very well," said the dog. "It's you're picture" and she went away. "No thank you" said the rabbit. I like it my way. Nobody's been* [inaudible]*."*

[pause]

Christine: Oh! I forgot to read. *The rabbit went on painting. Soon a came by. "No No No" said the bird. "The sun is too* [inaudible]*. Put in some more yellow.*

[pause]

That will make it orange." "No thank you" said Rabbit. I like it my way."

MH: Reading book please. [to Richard] Put your eraser away.

Christine: *"Well it's your picture," said the bird and she went away.*

MH: Sit down! [to Richard in a sharp tone]

David: *The rabbit went on painting. Soon a toad came along by. "O by* [restarts] *O my" said the toad.*

MH [to Samuel]: Now get your book out. You've got pencil, you've got eraser. You got everything you need to reeeead!

David: *"That water isn't right. It's too green. Put in more blue."* [pause] *Yikes. Everyone has something to say," said the rabbit. He went on painting just as a family of bugs came, came by.*

MH [to Samuel]: Do you need any of these to read? I doubt it.

Samuel: I, you, I need that. [pointing to assignment book]

MH: [sharply to Samuel] It's too late for that. You should have it down already. How do you even know where you read? Get your reading book out please.

David: *"Now what?" said that rabbit. "Wow" said the father bug. "Will you look at that" "Do you really think so?" said that rabbit. "Oh yes" said the bug. They* [inaudible] *"Yes" said the rabbit. "We'll, When it's your picture."*

Richard: [interrupts] Pic ture. Not pitcher.

MH: Shhhh! Go ahead.

MH: She did that so fast it's really kind of unreadable. [talking to Daisy who quietly approached Mrs. Hoffman to show her that she has finished correcting some 1st and 2nd grade worksheets]

Richard: Oops. [drops pencil]

Christine: *"I wonder how they will get it into their house," thought the rabbit.*

Richard: Green gob. That's what it looks like.

MH: Well how about using the next line? [to Christine who is stuck on a word]. Alright. Again tomorrow we're going to pick another story. Do your questions. You too Richard.

Richard: Yea!

This constitutes a 2nd grade reading class for David and Christine. In this we can see the general form of instruction in the form of "classes" as it applies to reading. Christine and David are highly aware of the routine. They come ready to read. They open their books. All Mrs. Hoffman does is ask Christine to start. We can see her initially try to ask some questions of Christine and David, apparently about getting them interested in the story, about beaches and painting colors. But these fade away and she seems to barely attend to anything other than whether the students are reading and taking their turns. Mrs. Hoffman later told me that she simply assumes that their reading aloud is their engagement in the text. We also see her attending to Richard and also to Samuel, who appears to annoy her in his confusion about what he should be doing.

While this class is going on Mrs. Hoffman is attending to at least three things that are evident (in this transcript). One, she sees and hears that David and Christine are doing their reading class properly. At Bighand students fulfill their roles in a reading class by taking turns reading aloud, most often alternating paragraphs but also alternating pages. Second, she is monitoring Richard, her ongoing discipline problem. Third, she is answering questions by at least two students not "in class," trying to make sure Samuel is on track and helping Daisy correct worksheets. Of primary importance here to Mrs. Hoffman is the stability of the class itself, what David and Christine are doing. It is as if at one point Mrs. Hoffman is not even needed. She starts out asking questions, that are tangentially related to the story (about beaches, etc.) and about how colors are made when combined and how these appear in the pictures in the chapter. But her own attention fades. We can also see Richard desperately trying to be involved in the interaction around this story, where he comments on colors in the picture and on beaches in Hawaii.[8]

I talked with David about this class later when he was at his desk. When I asked him if he considered the this reading class typical ("regular"), he responded affirmatively. "Just like most classes," he said. He looked at me as if I were quizzing him on something unique he may have missed and then said, "Except for Richard sitting there. He kept interrupting." When I asked why he kept reading if Richard bothered him, he said, "'Cuz I have to." I asked Christine the same questions about Richard, to which she simply shrugged her shoulders, "No big deal. Just read and get it over with. I ignore him."

What I think Christine and David are revealing is how the "class" form is a fully internalized routine. They carry on despite interruptions from Richard. I found myself wondering in my notes how an eight year old pays attention, to be "on task," well enough to block out Richard's actions, Mrs. Hoffman's sharp verbal responses to him and her audible interactions with Samuel and Daisy. David and Christine just carry on the "class" form and already in 2nd grade know how block to distractions, even those a couple of feet away.

In managing this reading "class" we see that Mrs. Hoffman makes some effort at responding to their reading (about beaches and colors). But this wanes and Christine and David read on. It is possible to see the powerful sway the routine class form has on these two students (who are in their third year at the school). Mrs. Hoffman's moves in and during this lesson are not geared toward either assessing student learning or cultivating meaning from the text, a common purpose assigned to students reading like this. She doesn't see her role as doing this. Rather, she takes students' progress through these stories, their completing written comprehension questions and the tests that accompany these textbook series as reliable proxies for reading achievement. Her teaching moves are primarily management-oriented and disciplinary in nature. It is as if the "classes" take care of themselves or, more accurately, the students take care of their portion of the "class" (taking turns reading), which is significant. Mrs. Hoffman can rely on the students to uphold this end of the work and she can thus tend to an unruly student and a confused first grader. The "class" is second nature to teacher and students and how they "do school" together.

One Afternoon's 5th Grade Math Class

Although Kimberly is the only fifth grader, Mrs. Hoffman still refers to Kimberly classes as "the fifth grade." Mathematics classes follow the same general pattern of all classes: students understand that they are to work quietly and independently on their assignments, hand those assignments into the teacher, come to class where Mrs. Hoffman informs the students of the acceptability of an assignment or test, be directed to proceed into the next assignment, have students read aloud directions and examples, and then return to one's desk in order to complete and "get through."

It is important to note that the mathematics curriculum for Bighand School is organized around two separate and very different math textbook series, Scott/Foresman & Co. and Saxon Publishing. Those of Scott/Foresman & Co. can be characterized as mainstream mathematics curricula that have some conceptual orientation. Saxon is characterized by isolated skills that recur, or "spiral," within separate lessons or units. The emphasis in Saxon Math is on repeated exercise or drill of skills. Mrs. Hoffman added the Saxon series the previous year at the urging of Stan Vogt, because he said ambiguously to her that "math was becoming important" with the coming of state standards. In effect, Bighand students are progressing through two different math programs simultaneously. And even though she has some reservations about Saxon Math, since "it is just too different" from Scott/Foresman, she views it as ultimately helpful in student achievement. Despite her reservations, Saxon Math is in actuality extraordinarily compatible with the system of classes at Bighand precisely because of the discrete, incremental repetitions and drill of the exercises and assignments. Math classes are thus geared around getting through these two textbook series. These series are not used in complementary fashion around particular mathematical concepts or as thematic resources, but as ends in themselves. This fits with Mrs. Hoffman's working belief in the educational benefit of quantity and saturation i.e., that simply more academic work will lead to more learning, or what she blithely calls "piling it on."

This fifth grade math class begins with Mrs. Hoffman calling Kimberly to the table. She simply starts by saying: "Page 253 for tomorrow. And that is more fractions and you have fractions on your test. Alright?" Kimberly responds, "OK." Standing about four and a half feet tall, Kimberly has a lanky and rail-thin preadolescent figure, with hands, feet and a toothy smile that look disproportionately large for her body. When she carries her books or a backpack, it is as if she is towing a third of her own weight. This contrasts with her deep, nasal, voice that sounds eerily like her mother's.

As Kimberly sits down, Mrs. Hoffman hands her the test she completed the day before, but she does not point out her grade (100%). Kimberly looks straight for the grade, marked in red at the top of the page. Kimberly makes a small smile of satisfaction as she sees this. "Page 253" refers to Kimberly's Scott/Foresman math textbook and the exercises on multiplication of fractions for the next day. She merely assumes that Kimberly knows what she needs to do. After tersely admonishing Richard, Mrs. Hoffman moves right on to the Saxon Math book.

5th Grade Reading Interaction

The transcript below of Kimberly's entire math class, approximately 5 minutes of interaction. Verbatim reading of the text is again indicated in italics.

Mrs. Hoffman: [to Richard] What did I say to do?! I won't say it again. Please. Richard sit down in your seat. I am going to have to write a note to mom if I do not see something happening here very soon. I am going to have to send home a report today. [to Kimberly] Simplifying decimal numbers. What does yours [book] say? Go ahead and read that. Mine [teacher's edition] says the same.

Kimberly: *When we write numbers, we should write them in the simplest form. When we simplify a number, we change the form of the number, but we do not change the value of the number. We learned how to simplify fractions by reducing. We can often simply.* [restarts] *We can often simplify decimal fractions as well.*

MH: [correcting] *numbers as well*

K: *numbers as well. We simplify decimal numbers by removing unnecessary zeros. We will explain this by simplifying, twenty ah, twenty-hundredths.*

MH: Right.

K: *The decimal number twenty-hundredths has a two in the tenth's place and a zero in the hundredths' place. The zeros in the hun-*

dredths' place mean no hundredths. If we remove the zero from twenty-hundredths, we get two-tenths. The number two-tenths also has a two in the tenths place and 'no hundredths.' Thu,

MH: [correcting] *Thus*

K: *Thus twenty hundredths...*

MH: Means "however." Twenty hundredths equals

K: *Twenty-hundredths equals two-tenths.*

MH: Even though we say it differently.

K: *That we say that twenty-hundredths simplifies to two-tenths. We can remove zeroes from the front of the whole numbers and from the back of the decimals numbers. We remove zeroes until we come back to a digit that is not a zero or until we come to a decimal point. Below we have simplified* [printed in book as 02.0100, 20.0, and 0.200] *zero two and one-hundred, twenty and zero tenths and two thousandths*

MH: *Two-hundred thousandths by removing*

K: *by removing the unnecessary zeros.*

MH: OK. *Simplify each decimal number* in [sample] number problems A through B. Do you have that?

K: Uh.

MH: Right there [pointing in K's book]. These seem to be the same [their books]. OK so what are we going to change this to? Three and

K: Three and two tenths. [printed in the book as 03.20]

MH: [Speaks quietly to herself as she writes down the pages of this assignment in her planbook for documentation of Kimberly's math work.]

MH: Alright. Sixth graders.

This comprises a fifth grade math class, "Simplifying Decimal Numbers" on this particular day. Mrs. Hoffman directs Kimberly to read the definitions and description of the Saxon Math "lesson." This lesson has no connection to the multiplication of fractions in Kimberly's Scott/Foresman textbook and test. She reads through orally the first of the four sample problems, to the satisfaction of Mrs. Hoffman. Mrs. Hoffman simply ends by marking in her planbook Kimberly's Saxon Math assignment and calls the 6th graders up for their math class. Kimberly returns immediately to her desk and quietly sets to work on her assignment. This class took around 5 minutes.

Unlike the 2nd grade reading class, we can see Mrs. Hoffman paying keen attention to Kimberly's reading of the definitions and descriptions of simplifying decimal numbers. She leads her through one example of simplifying decimal numbers and sends her on her way. Mrs. Hoffman told me after school that day that she did not prepare for Kimberly's class. She says she felt she really did not need to read ahead for this unit. It was simply and logically the next unit in what Mrs. Hoffman presumed was the correct order of math exercises and she felt she knew enough math to know what do (i.e., simplifying decimal numbers). This points to the faith she puts in these textbooks.

THE RECITATION AS A FUNCTIONAL TRADITION

This form of instruction exemplified in the reading and math classes, is highly effective when viewed against the local understandings of the purposes of education that lead Mrs. Hoffman to define her teaching problem in particular ways. In this locally important educational scheme, students must "get through" their textbooks in order to "keep up" with town school kids and demonstrate their readiness for secondary school. In this second grade reading class with David and Christine, we see that Mrs. Hoffman can rely on the class form to hold steady while she attends to at least two other students that are not involved in the current reading class. In a way, she is not really necessary. The key goal here is to have class, monitor student "progress" through the reading textbook and otherwise make sure they are advancing through the textbook series, that is getting through.

I cannot overemphasize how Mrs. Hoffman's teaching is organized around and driven by her goal to get students through these commercially produced textbook and workbook series. She has organized a highly systematic and, indeed, functional system of teaching with and through the textbooks and especially the recitations. She has defined the problem, taken on what she calls an "objective" and decontextualized program of study for each student (as defined by grade-level textbooks) and she has developed an extraordinarily effective system of teaching. These classes are elegant in their efficiency.

The old country school recitation involved the teacher calling upon individual and grade level groups of students (Cuban, 1994; Theobald, 1995). They often stood or sat on a hard bench. This instruction involved little more than the teacher lecturing and students reciting memorized passages or orally answering a series of teacher questions as directed by the teacher's textbook guide (Thayer, 1928). Student learning was determined through the accuracy of the recitation and appropriateness of responses to teacher questions. Students were then introduced to the next topic and their assignment in the textbook. And, they were expected to work quietly and individually on their preparations for recitations.

Here in Bighand School, it is possible to see the essential outline of this form of instruction. Most importantly, the textbook is still the unquestioned plan for curricular organization and student progress. Instead of orally quizzing students on whether they can recite a memorized text, or go through question-answer routines, Mrs. Hoffman relies on written performance on lessons and tests for indicators of student learning. Like the old recitation, she uses the class to introduce sequential topics in, and keeps track of student progress through, textbooks. Except the oral component does not involve memorization or right-answer responses, but a supervised or guided reading of printed text that introduces the student(s) to the next topic or lesson. The oral component is front-loaded in Mrs. Hoffman's scheme, to see if students understand what they are supposed to do, not what they have done, as represented in Kimberly's math class and David and Christine's reading class.

What is striking about this form of instruction is its sheer utility and refined functionality for this one-teacher setting, apropos Mrs. Hoffman's goal of getting students through a textbook-based curriculum so as to keep up and be ready for high school and middle school. It is a convention that helps Mrs. Hoffman organize her work with students and helps students to organize their own work. It requires a good deal of self-discipline on the part of the student. "Doing school" at Bighand, for the students, means continually keeping up with one's work, knowing that you will face the teacher regularly, and understanding that neither is a choice.

Doing classes is traditional in the sense that it resembles the old country school recitation in ways that may be even deeper than I first conjectured. In 1915 British educator Sara Burstall (1918) visited American schools and classrooms and noted "No impression of American education remains more vivid to the English acting teacher than that…embodied in the phrase 'recitation' used where we say lesson" (p. 156). She goes on to list her criticisms of this method, including an observation that

> the teacher appears to do too little; her share in the lesson is at a minimum…The teacher and the pupils are very much on level. She is not teaching them; she acts rather as chairman of a meeting, the object of which is to ascertain whether they have studied for themselves in a text-book…Clearly the master is the text-book, and here we strike on a vital peculiarity of American education. (pp. 158–159)

Burstall interprets that an American democratic ideal is the singular root cause for the recitation as she observed it. In retrospect, this is obviously an unfounded claim. However, her observations of the old recitation are prescient and point to the deeply rooted nature of the recitation and its modern form as I saw it at Bighand School. The image of the teacher as "chairman of a meeting" with textbooks and workbooks is an accurate description of teaching at Bighand School.

Classes at Bighand present themselves as common sense, or just the way things are done and have been done for ages in country schools. When I asked Mrs. Hoffman if she had considered organizing her curriculum in ways other than with classes like these, she shrugged her shoulders and looked nearly dumbfounded by the question. "I mean," she asked, "what other way can I do it?" Classes represent the most sensible way Mrs. Hoffman can conceive of her instruction. In chapter 5, I take up some of the broader symbolic function of this recitation pedagogy that further render this a sensible form of teaching. Mrs. Hoffman is implicitly drawing upon traditions of country school teaching to enact her pedagogy; her use of recitations makes perfect sense in the here and now as a functional instructional strategy.

NOTES

1. Mrs. Hoffman, her administrators and parents are all-reluctant to talk about this event and it is hard to place its significance for the current life of Bighand School. There are multiple versions of the event, but the basics include that a group of disgruntled parents were concerned with Mrs. Hoffman's demeanor (that she was rigid and unpleasant to the children) and that she did not have high academic expectations. In the end, there was a board meeting with parents and Mrs. Hoffman with Stan Vogt mediating. He discouraged a termination action, indicating that this would cost some legal fees in proper due process for a tenured teacher. There was also a preponderance of parents who supported Mrs. Hoffman, especially Molly's mother, and former students addressing the board in support of her, including Molly's brother. Ultimately, the problem was framed as an issue of accountability and documentation of students' academic work. The mediated agreement directed Mrs. Hoffman to document student academic work, which she does in great detail. She writes several times a day in her red plan book—before, during and after each class or recitation session— the students' progress through their textbooks and workbooks. In effect, one group of parents and Mrs. Hoffman won and she has stayed on since.

2. The county superintendent in Nebraska is a holdover from the 19th century, when the numerous small country districts made it impractical to have their own on-site administrators. The role exists as a result of state statute and is a county-wide elected, part-time position. With the effects of consolidation, i.e., large schools and school districts needing their administration, the role has become redundant. And Class One schools are required to contract with a certified administrator to fulfill various administrative duties (teach contracts, budgets, legal compliance, etc.). In 2000, Nebraska made the county superintendence optional, at the discretion of county boards of supervisors (who must pay for the superintendent). However, in many rural districts the county superintendent has remained implicated as a resource for the schools. It is up to the local school board to determine the extent of the involvement of the county superintendent. Bighand School's board looks favorably upon Mr. Vogt as an experienced administrator who is there

to help when asked. He informed me that he saw one of his jobs to help a district stay open if the local community desired and it was fiscally feasible.

3. The Educational Service Units (ESU) in Nebraska are intermediate public educational agencies that provide supplementary educational services to K–12 school districts, including special education. They take on special importance for Class One schools and rural districts that do not have in-service infrastructures those large, organized districts have. There are nineteen ESUs in the state that cover areas roughly determined by population's density (e.g., Lincoln Public Schools has its own ESU due to the large number of students enrolled in the district).

4. The only out of date textbook I could see was a 6th grade social studies textbook that still had Eastern Europe designated as Soviet.

5. At the time I was sitting on my son's school district's community curriculum council, which is a parent advisory group, and one of the things were asked to evaluate and offer input was on the district's choice between one of three reading textbook series from major publishers. I was overwhelmed with the consistency of the series and saw this was a choice between three of the same thing. They were different on the surface; graphics, etc. but were remarkably uniform on the overall style, form and content. I voted for the one that had the nicest pictures and most representations of people of color.

6. Older students will occasionally help younger students, invariably some assignment from a textbook or a workbook, such as listening to them read. But Mrs. Hoffman considers this a distraction and peripheral to the importance of classes.

7. By my count, as they appeared in my field notes, I observed over 500 "classes" either directly sitting at Mrs. Hoffman's table or indirectly from across the room as I sat next to students (my interest was in how they viewed the classes when seated at their desks). Mrs. Hoffman was reluctant to let me tape record these classes and was clearly uncomfortable with my request. She finally allowed me to after I pleaded with her that the best way to accurately represent the classes was through verbatim transcripts.

8. As a former teacher, these efforts by Richard were painful for me to watch. He really seemed to be longing to be involved in the interaction. But, it is important to recall that from Mrs. Hoffman's point of view, her major concern was to diminish his disruption, both in class and for other students who are, after all, required to be working quietly. Mrs. Hoffman expressed to me her concern that if Richard were involved and that if responded to all his questions and comments that this would be time taken away from the "actual" work of the reading class, that there would be too much "talk instead of reading." She fears she might be encouraging the unruly behavior that she is seeking to undermine, since this hampers "getting through."

REFERENCES

Burstall, S.B. (1909). *Impressions of American education in 1908*. New York: Longmans, Green and Co.

Cuban, L. (1994). *How teachers taught: Constancy and change in American classrooms.* New York: Teachers College Press.

Geertz, C. (1983a). Common sense as a cultural system. *Local knowledge. Further essays in interpretive anthropology* (pp. 55–72). NY: Basic Books.

Geertz, C. (1983b). "From the native's point of view": On the nature of anthropological understanding. *Local knowledge. Further essays in interpretive anthropology* (pp. 72–93). NY: Basic Books.

Kliebard, H. (1986). *The struggle for the American curriculum, 1893–1958.* Boston: Routledge & Kegan Paul.

Marshall, J. (1989). The picture. In D. Alvermann, *My best hear hug (Health Reading Series. Level 1).* (pp. 23–39). Lexington, MA: D.C. Heath & Co.

Senk, S.L., & Thompson, D.R. (Eds.) (2002). *Standards-based school mathematics curricula: What are they? What do students learn?* Mahwah, NJ: Lawrence Erlbaum.

Thayer, V. (1928). *The passing of the recitation.* Boston: D. C. Heath.

Theobald, P. (1995). *Call school: Rural education in the Midwest to 1918.* Carbondale: Southern Illinois University Press.

Wilson, S. (2003). *California dreaming: Reforming mathematics education.* New Haven: Yale University.

CHAPTER 5

LEARNING TO THINK
AT UPPER RILL SCHOOL

This chapter describes the teaching practices at Upper Rill School. With its eight students, grades one through eight, Will Tomlinson considers the school's size and continuity of student enrollment generative and flexible. Subject matter and grade levels are regularly integrated though common curricula. Specific instances of instruction are examined in Will's adoption of the Junior Great Books literature series. The teacher works to organize subject matter thematically to connect all students around an idea, e.g., the mathematics theme of patterns. Instruction is carried out in "conversations" with individuals, same grade and mixed grade groups of students. Upper Rill's teacher has gained community support for what he calls a curriculum of "learning to think." This pedagogy has emergent qualities of progressive instruction, contingent with a modified improvisation, and is modestly student-centered.

WILL'S DEFINED PEDAGOGICAL TASK

Like Mrs. Hoffman, Will Tomlinson is presented with the age-old problem of a country school teacher: how to organize curriculum and instruction to accommodate ten different children, at seven different grade levels that is agreeable to the school's board, the principal, parents and his own sense of

Naturally Small: Teaching and Learning in the Last of the One-Room Schools, pages 59–96

a good education that involves what he calls "learning to think"? Will describes his challenges in the following way:

> Well, this can be complicated. I want the kids to learn how to think, and not become stupid or make decisions that are stupid, or unwise I should say...I think about a kid like Nate, for instance, who can be incredibly smart in math and science, but will make dumb decisions and I'm afraid of that carrying over into academics...he gets frustrated in one area and that will work its way into things he can do well when he applies himself, like math. So I have to figure out things to do to help them to think, which is not always easy...This is why...we do a lot of things together and...talking about things, thinking through them, see them thinking through them...otherwise, I'm not a hundred percent sure [that they are thinking], not that I am anyway. [laughs]

When I asked him about the need to inform the board and parents about students' progress, he responded:

> I suppose I've got to use some textbooks and some standardized curriculum materials, to a certain extent, and obviously doing alright on the MAT test.[1] They have got to know if their kids are at grade level. Cal [the principal] wants that too, a kind of guarantee that they are not behind when they go to middle school or to high school. I think he sells the school on this...Not everything can be fun and games and not everything is one big school project, everybody doing the same thing, obviously. So I kind of take that as a given.

Will's definition of his work entails a tension between what counts as a successful student and a worthwhile educational experience. Being at grade level and learning to think are not inherently complimentary and are certainly potentially contradictory. A teacher doing what it takes to get students to think may not be harmonious with what a teacher needs to do to have them be at grade level, particularly as this is defined as completion of standardized, textbook-based curricula and when performance on standardized testing is used as a proxy for learning. Yet these are the primary expectations that Will interprets as defining his task as a teacher and these shape the actions he takes in the organization of curriculum and teaching. As he says, he has to "figure out things to help them think" while ensuring that students are "at grade level."

Role of the Principal

These expectations are shaped significantly by the school's contracted principal, Cal Booker. In addition to Upper Rill School, Cal is the principal for four other Class One school districts in the area. Cal sees "being at grade level" as a matter of Upper Rill School's survival. Along with the school board, Cal views the need to enroll a minimum number of students in order to have the per pupil costs in apparent parity with the affiliated K–12 district. Their goal is twelve students. The costs of running a Class One is public knowledge in the affiliated district(s) that would absorb the students and the local school revenue and a recalculated portion of state aid if the school were to close. And the superintendent of Portage Schools, Upper Rill's only affiliated K–12 district, is vocal about his desire to see Upper Rill close down and acquire its school property tax revenue. Consequently, Cal and the board agree that they need to make an effort to show their own community, and the surrounding communities, that they are not a "luxury school" for a few children. Since it is not reliable to assume that there will be enough children in the district in any given school year to reach twelve, and that those in the district will themselves enroll, recruiting children from families who reside outside of the district is a now a major concern for the board and Cal. In order to recruit students, Cal determines that there needs to be assurance of students being at grade level. More generally, as a supporter of Class One schools, Cal wants to be able to claim to anyone inside or outside the school district that the students are at grade level and that they do not get behind.

However, it is important to note that Cal does not see this as an end in itself, as the administrators at Bighand School do (as part of keeping up and being ready). This is not, for him, primarily an issue about being prepared for high school or middle school. Cal assumes that when students leave Upper Rill that they are prepared. Rather, "being at grade level," sits at the top of an array of values of Class One schools generally, and Upper Rill in particular, that he seeks to promote and display. These values are in a brochure (see Figure 5.1) that Cal created in order to promote and "sell" the school to parents who might option their children to Upper Rill. As Cal explains:

> We have to tell these parents that nothing is lost here, that their kids will in no way be behind when compared to a graded school, that they will not lose out. But this is a negative— what *won't* happen to kids here. We need to promote the positive, what *will* happen, and why we should keep a Will Tomlinson in business. Parents need to hear this before we can talk about all the good things and benefits of the school…like the strong, multi-age instructional groups that you see whenever you walk in here, *and that kids just really like being here*…especially when a one-room school is foreign to [most parents]. All they have are images from TV and books about one-room schools, and these are always old and outdated (emphases in his).

Consequently, for "parents who naturally ask if their kid is at grade level," Cal indicates that "we need to tell them this, they need to hear it…if we want these schools to survive" since they offer a unique alternative to the large graded school systems with which he is familiar and experienced (Cal was a principal at a large high school in United a decade earlier).

Quality K–8 Education!

Upper Rill Schools Offer:

- Experienced teaching staff
- Low student/teacher ratio: 7/1
- Individualized Instruction
- High standards for student behavior
- Ongoing teacher–parent contact
- Education presented as a team effort of staff, parents, and students
- Board is interactive with the community
- Quality special education services

Focus on Student Learning!

- Parents report children enjoy coming to school
- Individualized student attention promotes learning
- Strong teacher–parent relationship promotes learning
- Our students are consistently achieving test scores that exceed the national C.A.T. average test scores
- High expectations for student behavior improves student self-discipline
- Individualized music instruction
- Integrated curriculum weaving current events in with basic instruction

School Structure

- Students work in interdisciplinary groups
- Multi-age instructional groups designed to provide the best researched based instruction
- Instructional areas combined when appropriate to provide students a more complete learning opportunity
- Conveniently located just seven miles west of Lincoln

Come join our school community!

Figure 5.1.   Upper Rill brochure.

While this has much in common with Bighand School's sense of purpose, it differs significantly as this is the "given" that makes other things possible— "all the good things and benefits of the school." "Being at grade level" is the structural *sine qua non* for Will at Upper Rill.

From Will's point of view, it is as if Cal is setting out an implied bargain: *if you help me ensure parents and the board that students are at grade level, I will offer you autonomy and support to pursue innovations that are unique to one-room schools and make them special.*[2] This bargain significantly shapes how Will sees what he must do *and* what he can do at Upper Rill.

There are two important aspects to Cal's "hands off" approach. One, this lets Will determine how to get his students to stay on grade level:

> I tell Will that the kids need to be at grade level, but I do not tell him how to do it. My philosophy of these [one-teacher] schools is to find the best people [teachers] and let them go to town. Leave them alone. "You figure it out since you are here and the expert. That's why we hired you." The moment I tell them what they need to do in designing their curriculum is the moment we lose what is good about these places.

When I asked Cal if there was not a contradiction to what he says about making public assurances of students being at grade level and his professed commitment to teacher autonomy, that the former required diminishing the latter, he responded:

> I get what you are saying. Is there a contradiction or, worse, a deception? But I see it as kind of laying down a law, if you will—I'm a lawyer and can't help it—like speeding on the highway. You have to follow the law and not be reckless, what everyone expects of the other drivers on the road, but I am not going to sit next to you every time you get behind the wheel of a car. Telling parents that their kids are at grade level is the very least we can ask of any teacher, don't you think? They're worried about their kids. And rightly so. But, how you do that and get there is another matter...I try to let the teacher dictate to me, to tell me how they can get there and try to help them do that...Otherwise we lose out on the best these places have to offer by simply doing the same-old same-old, which you can get anywhere at any school...and that would be sad.

Second, Cal makes what he calls a "leap of faith," that "sometimes lets me down," in what he sees as valuable and unpredictable educational practices that can "spring from these places." These teaching practices and activities contribute to what he calls a "more whole" learning experience. Cal is imprecise, and uses unspecified examples of what he means, but namely curricular and pedagogical practices that he claims are not part of everyday life in large, graded schools, such as students working in interdisciplinary and cross age groups ("more like a family, which is the way most of us learned before school"), the greater opportunity for inclusion of all children in activities, how students are encouraged to "discipline themselves," rather than being policed by teachers, programs and public demonstrations (e.g., Christmas and spring programs) that involve all students substantially, and that children simply enjoy coming to school. "How can you," he asks rhetorically, "order a teacher to do something when he knows the kids and knows how to use the [one-teacher] context? You've *got* to assume they know what they're doing" (emphasis his).

Will's Teaching Expectations

It is easy to romanticize Cal as a heroic administrator for Class One schools, at least as far as teachers are concerned. For Will, he is indeed "a 'teacher's principal' who stands by you." And Cal indicates a nuanced understanding of any instructional policy (explicit or implicit), i.e., that teachers are the agents of any policy and they cannot be controlled entirely, and is it probably unwise, if not impractical, to do so anyway. But Cal's stance is important not simply for its expressed confidence in the small, country school teacher. More significant to this analysis is how Cal's expectations shape how Will sees his work, what he thinks he needs to do and what he sees he can do in his implied bargain, especially as this interacts with Will's working philosophy of "learning to think." Will is embedded effectively in two sets of pedagogical expectations that shape how he defines his pedagogical challenge. One is drawn directly from his administrator, about students at grade level. Will assents to this expectation; he deadpans, "It's just something that I have to do and it's not that hard to do. I live with it." What is important to note here is that while Will is provided the autonomy to get students to grade level as he sees fit, this is not accompanied by a concealed expectation that Will "align" his curriculum with the affiliated high school district in Benefit. Nor does Cal expect that Will comply with curricula of other Class One schools in the he county.[3] If Will chooses an alignment, then Cal supports this, but the assumption is that Will determines his own "route" to "grade level."

The other expectation emerges from Will's desire to get kids to think, occasioned by the autonomy provided in this small setting and his administrator. Will interprets the autonomy given to him by Cal as a warrant to pursue forms of instruction and curricula beyond those that are pragmatically directed at getting students to be at grade level, beyond what is offered by some form of standardization, e.g., via textbooks. Thus Will's view of his work, and the practices that flow from it, are shaped and constrained most immediately by his principal, who is both the "chief enforcer," according to the School Board treasurer, and who Will says is "my greatest advocate" with both parents and the school board.

Operating Philosophy: Learning to Think

When I asked Will about his beliefs and ideals in teaching, he is rather reticent, as if somehow embarrassed by a lack of an articulated systematic view about what he believes in and is seeking to accomplish at the school. His words do not appear in the aforementioned brochure. But he does state resolutely that his primary goal can be summed up in the phrase, "Getting kids to think." As he says:

> I want kids to know about something and what lies behind it, *why* something is the way it is. I want them to do more than just get through the assignments, not just spit back answers. It's about the *why*. Figuring out why means having to think hard and not be lazy. This is not something that not kids come to school with, some more than others (emphases his).

This working philosophy for Will is rooted in his disillusionment with schooling as a mindless activity, places where "kids are not thinking" and "making decisions that are stupid" or decisions that "make them look stupid." For Will, making decisions has life consequences. "If you start making stupid decisions when you are young," he declares, "then you will do this later on, and that can get you in trouble." The world can be a threatening place, according to Will, and stupidity cannot help. Whenever Will talks about this, he almost always begins to drop the idiomatic "stupid" and begins to employ the terms "wise" and "intelligent," as if he becomes aware how crude his own words sound. When I asked him if he meant that by making "stupid" decisions students can effectively make themselves "unintelligent," Will responded, "That's it. Make enough dumb decisions and you will not be intelligent. That's no way to go through life."

Will's words sound unrefined, even inarticulate, for a teacher who is concerned with thinking. Indeed, they appeared so to me when I first heard him speak this way.[4] And as banal as they sound, they represent a view that animates his teaching practice, and I return to this later. He bemoans that the bulk of his own teacher education was built around writing lesson plans and "using the latest jargon" like "whole language." He jokes that there was a string of contradictions in his teacher education program. For instance, on the one hand, his professors preached a supposedly complex, "constructivist" learning theory, that implies thinking. On the other hand, they emphasized a behaviorist model of curriculum built around highly specified lesson planning, with "student will" statements, thus focusing on students' behavior rather than their thinking or sensemaking.

Will is indeed pointing out a seriously glossed-over contradiction present in his teacher education program and in a good deal of district-level policy. Focusing on student thought processes and focusing on their getting through lessons are clearly not the same thing. In his teacher education program he quips, "Madeleine Hunter was king."[5] He notes that precise lesson planning, advanced in his teacher education program, "leaves the illusion that you know what is exactly going to happen for each kid, for each lesson, for each day, for each unit...That's ludicrous. Just doing something on a worksheet does not mean they learn anything." It appears that Will conscientiously avoids using educational reform argot, preferring to figure out how to enact a curriculum of "thinking" and using unpolished, or at least non-academic, language to describe that.

ORGANIZATION OF TEACHING AND CURRICULUM AT UPPER RILL

To deal with this two-fold definition of his work—getting students at grade level and getting them to think—Will engages a hybrid of practices and resources. His practices are an admixture individualized, conventional textbook-based curriculum and some more ambitious instruction that is conversation-based, directed at "getting them to think" and exploiting the diversity of ages. Like Mrs. Hoffman, Will employs conventional grade-level textbooks and workbooks as devices for grade-level organization of curriculum in reading, social studies, and especially math. Science also had textbooks, but over 90% of his science curriculum is derived from packaged projects, from multiple sources, some of which are textbooks, and projects such as units from the a state natural history museum on owls, weather observation and AIMS[6] activities. For Will, usage of textbooks accomplishes two things. For one, he sees them as a way for him to have some general idea of students' progress in their respective grade levels. This is important because, as described below, the students frequently interact around common activities and common readings such as the Junior Great Book series and science projects, such as local weather tracking. Second, it is a marker for parents; Will can explain to parents where their children are at academically, "I can get a sense of where kids are at and I can tell the parents that. Pretty basic."

However pragmatic this is, something in the usage of textbooks and standardized curricula nags Will. He regularly notes to me his concern for there being "something better" that "gets kids to think, not just do the worksheet." He indicates that this not only interferes with students' learning, by "locking them into a pattern...of moving ahead no matter what" that they may not have learned or mastered the "objectives," but for himself and his planning. "I don't buy," he says, "that you can completely predict, like [with] Madeleine Hunter lesson plans. What if I need to change something, or modify things? I can't be locked in." Will is expressing his mistrust of the sense of certainty that precise lesson planning offers, that a teacher cannot predict ahead of time whether and how students are learning in any particular activity or assignment. For Will, this contrasts starkly with his own thinking about what he can do and especially as he tries to craft a curriculum that gets students to think. Though Will does not explicitly say so, his own thinking about curriculum is tied to his students' thinking.

Moreover, Will has concerns about how precise planning can lead to excessively separating students into individual work activities. "I've come to learn that kids can work well together, that there is something beneficial in it." Will is similarly imprecise about what these benefits are. For him it seems "almost unnatural to keep students apart" in their activities. His view seems to flow not so much from a teaching ideal, though it may have become one for Will. Rather, having students work together seems borne out of his experience that students can do so readily *and* that separating students is complicated and, therefore, impractical; "keeping each one busy" is "just a planning nightmare." Plus, there are management and disciplinary advantages "where I don't have to always be looking over my shoulder to make sure so-and-so is doing his work and that so-and-so is doing hers." When I ask Will if this is a matter of older kids being able to look out for or supervise younger ones, he replied, "That's pretty much it. The Erecksens are fine. Danielle and Nora can take over, and Nate knows the drill. Mary will take care of Anna. Scott will do that too. In fact, they [the Erecksens] all do. Even Marlon will read for Danny." Subsequently, Will asks rhetorically, "Why not let them work together...when they can learn just as well from each other than me? I just gotta let it go" (laughing).

Consequently, the textbooks are for Will a loose guide for curriculum organization for individual students as much as they are potential disruptions in getting kids to think and in their working together. He prefers to have students work cooperatively in activities and consequently he is continually considering how he can use textbooks, workbooks and activities as common curricula, even with children across vast grade levels. When, for instance, the 6th grade social studies textbook (Scott's) had a unit on bananas, then bananas became (and how they are berries from a grass) the social studies activity for the day with the 6th grade worksheet supplemented with some internet search. Will determines that there needs to be a proper mixture of older and younger students working together so that they all can complete the activity and the questions on the worksheet. He sees a natural break among the K–2 student and the 4th–8th graders. Similarly, for his literature units, while there is a fourth grade level story from the literature series, the 4th, 5th, 6th, 7th and 8th grade students will read it and participate in the discussion of the story, and sometimes the 2nd graders, as in the example of the story *Wisdom, Wages, Folly Pay* described below.

Will tells that he thinks of his planning in one to two week "chunks" of time. This is a pragmatic time figure that allows him attend to student progress through the textbooks and put into place projects and adjust the literature of the newly adopted Junior Great Books. Students get though particular sets of tasks, units often related to the standardized curriculum material but which he leaves open-ended for activities and improvisation with worksheets and common activities. Moreover, it is the multi-age cross interaction that he is interested in using and exploiting when possible.

SCHOOL DAYS

Flowing from Will's working philosophy, and his coping with the small and multiage setting, instruction is carried out with individual students, small same-age (e.g., Mary/Marlon and Dylan/Penny) and multi-age groups. Instruction occurs mainly while students and Will are at their desks, in a large triangle, with Will occupying his own corner (see Figure 5.2 for classroom map), sometimes they sit across from him in the chairs immediately in front of his desk. To outsiders like me this all seems rather "laid back," as if Will were presiding over a series of ongoing seminars and students off on their own. However, when students work on projects or play board games

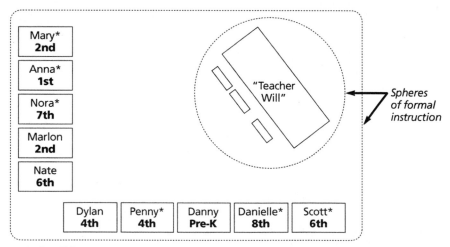

* Erecksen Siblings

Figure 5.2.   Classroom seating arrangement, top floor at Upper Rill school.,

they sit at tables toward the back of the top floor room or in the basement (where they have lunch).

There is no typical day at Upper Rill, just as there is no typical week, though there are days that are typically Upper Rill. To gain some sense of the flow of curriculum and instruction in a school day, it is helpful to look across some randomly selected days (see Tables 5.1 and 5.2). There is no posted schedule in the school (which is in violation of Nebraska law for Class One schools). Entering the school, at any given time during a school day, one will find Will leading the students through a common math problem (such as "magic squares,"[7] one of Will's favorite things to do); or working with Danny one on one at his desk, helping him write his letters or

Table 5.1. Friday, November 5, 2999 Schedule at Upper Rill

Time	Activity
8:35 AM	Literature Junior Great Books Danielle reading downstairs to Anna, The Shoemaker and the Elves. Nora reading aloud downstairs to Marlon and Mary, The Magic Listening Cap. Teacher Will in conversation with Penny, Dylan, and Scott and Nate about the story *The Little Humpbacked Horse.*
9:00	Nora, Marlon, and Mary finish Danielle and Anna finish. Anna reads silently at her desk. Nora works on a her crossword puzzle (she is creating it for spelling) at her desk. Mary is reading silently at the back table. Danielle searching library for a book. Marlon reading alone by the fish tank.
9:45	Recess
10:15	Teacher Will resumes conversation with Penny, Dylan, and Scott and Nate, the s story *The Little Humpbacked Horse.* All others resume individual reading.
10:38	Danielle and Nora join in the conversation with Penny, Dylan, and Scott and Nate, the story *The Little Humpbacked Horse.*
11:00	Danielle's science lesson (for all students) downstairs, "Will Saturn Float in a tub of water?"
11:35	Lunch
12:45 PM	Resume Danielle's science lesson—activity weighing displaced water.
2:30	Music (Caroline Erecksen is music teacher)
3:25	Get ready to leave

Table 5.2.   Thursday, February 24, 2000 Schedule at Upper Rill

Time	Activity?????
8:35 AM	Erecksens not here yet (uncharacteristic, they are always punctual).
	Marlon is sitting with Danny in the stuffed chair, reading to him the story *Why the Opossum in Gray.*
	Nate reading marine biology book by himself.
8:39	Erecksens arrive. Teacher Will informs that since the traveling special education teacher is coming to work with Wane today, that the student have until 9:00 to clean out their desks and then read quietly or do other work.
8:40	Dylan arrives (not uncommon for him to be late)
8:45	Mary takes out a shell fossil from the classroom collection and starts to scrape off the dirt. Marlon comes over and helps.
9:00	Spec. Ed. teacher arrives and begins work with Nate at the back table.
	Teacher Will has math activity worksheets "Animal Antics" and Animal Kingdoms" Student work in pairs: Dylan (4th) & Mary (2nd); Marlon (2nd) & Penny (4th); Nora (7th) & Danny (pre-K); Scott (6th) & Anna (1st grade).
10:00	Recess. Kickball.
10:45	Anna helps Danny write his letters ("He stops way J").
	Mary and Marlon working in math textbook, separately but occasionally conferring on multiplication.
	Scott, Dylan and Nate and Penny are reading *Time* [Magazine] *For Kids.*
11:00	Anna doing a math test.
11:30	Lunch/Recess. Basketball
1:00 PM	Students resume the works they were doing prior to lunch.
1:30	Board games: *War* for Nate, Nora, Scott, and Danny; *Clue* for Dylan, Marlon, Penny, Mary
	Anna reading by herself.
1:30	Teacher Will hands out math worksheets for each student from their respective grade level textbook series. He has group and individual meetings with students on their math.
2:00	Teacher Will hands out worksheet to everyone pertaining to the Junior Great Book series one "good pride" vs. "bad pride" from the level 4 series story *How the Tortoise Became.*
2:20	Teacher Will leads a discussion of the worksheet good pride vs. bad pride, asking students to look of evidence in the text for the following day's discussion.
3:25	Get ready to leave.

additions facts; Robbie sitting with Amy in the soft chair reading a Dr. Suess book with Anna; if weather permits, a game of modified kickball on the basketball court so that Anna and Danny can play; Will directing Dylan and

Penny through their social studies textbook and questions; a session of "court" when one student believes that another student has violated some rule (the infringement is often unsportsmanlike conduct during recess); or Will leading "gym class" by having student do their *kata* (movement forms from martial arts). The only predictable schedule items in the week and in the day of Upper Rill are morning and afternoon recesses, music on Fridays (2:00 or 2:30 PM, taught by Nicole Erecksen), individual spelling tests on Monday mornings, and lunch (around 11:25 AM).

Everyday Rules and Control

While the schedule may not be obviously predictable, there are predictable, shared expectations and local rules of and for student conduct in the school in and around academic work. Daily life is not a constant academic reinvention at Upper Rill for Will and especially not for the students. It is extremely rare to see overt student resistance at the school (acting out, refusing teacher requests, etc.). Ultimately the students have a shared understanding that they are to actively, as Nate says, "do our work, or else," and participate in cooperative activities. And when a student is not doing something sanctioned by the teacher or not working at the assigned activity, Teacher Will immediately sees this. This is itself an immediate function of the small space they inhabit together. The students understand this surveillance and how it plays into the rule of ultimate deferral to the teacher. And when a student does not know what to do, the rule is that the student must go to Teacher Will to figure out what to do. The students come to understand the "flow" of the day and a week, as Teacher Will says. What appear to be unstructured days composed of unstructured activities are, in effect, highly organized in terms of the implied rules and students' shared understanding of what they are supposed to be doing. Nora puts it this way:

> We have our work that we are suppose to do, like our math assignments and reading assignments in Great Books, et cetera, et cetera. When Will tells us to work on something, we do it. Like, sometimes I help Anna. And Will, like, then tells us to stop because we are going to do a project or talk about a story [e.g., Junior Great Books], or do some math on the board, or do a worksheet word problem, yadayadayadayada.

Despite the lightness of her comments (she looked at me with raised eyebrows as if she thought I was asking about the obvious), it is the very lightness with which she says these that points to the deeply established nature of schooling, school interaction, and understandings of student obligation at Upper Rill. Nora, like all students, has individual work to do. More significant is her deferral to Will when he informs students of non-individual activities, e.g., those that include working with and cooperating with others. Students are obligated to follow Will's direction to shift to cooperative activities. As Nate says:

> We have to do what Will tells us to do...even if it is working with the little kids who bug me sometimes. You have to do *something*, like your assignments, until Will says its okay to play a game or go outside [for recess]. Something I don't like is having to talk a lot 'cuz its embarrassing. But I have to, in front of everybody! He's always asking us *why why why*! Sometimes we don't know! (emphases his)

Nate says these things with a smile and a laugh. As noted, Will considers him the "veteran" or "senior" at the school since, even though Nora and Danielle are older, Nate has been at the school longer than any other student. He is also quietly referring to his speech impediment which becomes apparent when he is anxious, but is hardly detectable otherwise. It is the public nature of the school interaction, the expectation that he will have to "talk" and interact with others in shared work that Nate is referring to.

He is indicating, like Nora, the obligation that is established at the school for students to not only do what Will tells them to, but that this includes "working with others." Students at Upper Rill internalize the idea that they will be expected to work together and that this can happen when Will directs them to. Reciprocally, this is something that Will has created as a pedagogical right, to not only ask students to do their work, but to do this cooperatively. It is part of the unstated cultural feature of Upper Rill that students automatically work together when asked; it's just the way it is, just as classes are just the way it is at Bighand, so is working together when the teacher directs students to do so. Therefore, this rule does not appear as orders or commands from a superior, since working together involves the students willful assent to "work." Rather, it is "how things are done here" that emerge as a course of redundant activity than compose local cultural patterns of everyday life at the school.

When I asked the students if there was a conflict between working together when they are told to and when they want to, their answer is invariable. "We have to. You just can't refuse," says Danielle, "That would be insubordination! [laughing]. You just gotta and it isn't *that* bad" (emphasis hers).

What this points to is that instruction at Upper Rill takes place in a context composed of rights and duties that are habit, or second nature, to the students, internalized rules that are rarely addressed openly by Will. It indicates a kind of underlying control that Will has established at the school and the confidence he enjoys in that control when he enacts *any* curriculum activity or innovation. The control is nearly invisible to the casual observer because it is embedded in the "laid back" environment. Students simply do not challenge or resist. It's like the air—just there, part of the environment and taken in by the students to the point where it becomes a subconscious part of their school existence. And their parents see the outcome of these rules and Will's control as a disciplined environment. *All* the parents I interviewed said this was a value of the school, even if they do not fully understand how this is created and sustained. Significantly, Will's widely distributed control allows and is implicated in his capacity to take on new kinds of teaching.

INSTANCES OF UPPER RILL PEDAGOGY

I want to highlight one end of Will's pedagogical spectrum that most fully symbolizes his aspiration to enact a curriculum of "learning to think" and that is clearly enabled by the small environment. Just as there are certainly other areas of his practice worth focusing upon, my concerns are specifically directed at how he conscientiously organizes instruction to take into account the small multi-age setting. These are the occasions when a majority of the students engage in common activities and are all part of the same conversation. This area of his practice is in reading, or literature, with his newly adopted Junior Great Books. Like Mrs. Hoffman, Will was reluctant to have me audio-tape record his instruction, though we agreed at the outset of my project that I could do this with his consent. Will's teaching of Junior Great Books was the area he said he felt most comfortable with my recording. This came about after I told him that I thought that his teaching of the Junior Great Books best represents what he aspires to as a teacher, the improvisational give and take of conversation-based teaching that expresses his "getting them to think." I told Will that I thought this was the most unique part of his teaching that really set him apart from other one-room school teachers and is connected to what I am ultimately concerned with in my study, the relationship of teaching practices to the small scale setting of the country school. He let me turn on the tape recorder for 6 separate story units. I have selected events built around a 6th grade story, *Gaston*, and a 4th grade story *Wisdom's Wages Folly's Pay* for closer examination of how Will uses a conversation-based pedagogy in his effort to fulfill his personal pedagogical goal of getting his students to think.

I should say at the outset that I am not seeking to do a literacy or literary analysis. Nor am I seeking to hold up either the Junior Great Books, or Will's teaching of them, as some ideal or model for literature or literacy instruction in one-room or large graded schools. Nor do I make claims as to whether the Junior Great Books actually leads to higher literacy rates (i.e., that students are above and beyond grade level; I leave it to the standardized test scores and assumptions of Cal that this is so). Rather, in these lessons we see most clearly Will's efforts at using the multi-age setting, the flexible schedule he operates, the subtle but very strong control he can exert and what is by all indications the most enjoyable part of his teaching. And it is here where school size matters and comes into relief apropos his pedagogical efforts. His instruction reflects almost unconsciously and certainly unintentionally the kind of ambitious teaching that some literacy reformers call for. Moreover, because the Great Books series is new to Will and his students this year, it is in these excerpts from the story unit that we can see Will and the students learning how to "do" Junior Great Books.

Adopting Junior Great Books

Will adopted the Junior Great Books (JGB) series in the fall of 1999 as part of his reading and literature curriculum. He informs that he has always been quietly frustrated with what he determines is low quality literature in the commercially produced basal (textbook) readers. He still uses these for supplementary reading and as indicators of students' progress and if they are at grade level. For him the basal stories were weak and not conducive to thinking and learning about "why things happen the way they do" in literature. As Will puts it, "I want them to look beyond what the plot is, who did what and when, and so on." Will does not express any particular theory of literature that he works from, such as "reader response," nor New Criticism,[8] or literacy for that matter, such as "whole language," though he is clearly aware of whole language via his own teacher education (and the teacher educator that promoted it, whom he came to dislike intensely) and he ridicules phonics-based instruction. Nor does he propound any political stance, from the culture wars, over the preference for a "canon" of great Western literature, implied by the very name "*Great* Books."

However, Will does have a belief that there is better and worse literature and that there are better and worse ways to engage children in literature. It does reflect his concern that students have "something better" than the basal readers that he finds to have simplistic stories, thus implicitly insulting the reader, "treating them like they cannot understand much," or that they cannot think through things. But, he says, "I still use them though; they are not completely worthless." He is inexact about what he considers better literature and literature instruction. He effectively considers "better" when children can extemporaneously talk about a story or a text after having read it or heard it. "Answering questions at the end of the chapter is just too simple," he says. "They should be able to think on their feet." His view is both a reaction against basal readers and the mass produced textbooks that try to please as wide an audience as possible and the taking of a stand on quality literature, i.e., what counts as "great." It is the taking of a stand on quality that Will admires: "someone, somewhere is saying what is good literature. Like, I know that Dostoevsky is a great author."

The assumption of a possible canon comforts Will in this choice, and he assents to the JGB as embodying a canon. But it is not an ill-informed or capricious assent to so-called "greatness" of JGB. Will indicates that he was always interested in literature. When I first met him two years earlier and visited his school, I witnessed his students in their spring program enacting a "coffeehouse conversation" (that they wrote) on the connections between *Cat in the Hat* (and his nihilistic tendencies) and a short story by Dostoevsky. Whether Will's assessment is accurate about basal readers being less substantive is not something I take up. Rather, it is important to view that he interpreted an opportunity to do something better and felt he could carry that out at Upper Rill in the classroom environment over which he enjoys considerable social control. He came upon the JGB by accident, when he received a promotional letter and brochure in the mail in spring, 1999. Will convinced Cal and his board to purchase the series. He traveled to Omaha to attend the Junior Great Books workshop early in the fall, 1999 and started using the series immediately.

The Junior Great Book Series is the school version of the Great Books Foundation program for adult readers. Begun fifty years ago, the goal of the program was for adults to have a way to read and discuss the so called "great works" of western literature. As indicated in their website, the Foundation describes as its goal, "to instill the habits of mind that characterize a self-reliant thinker, reader, and learner." Their description goes on to say that "Great Books programs are predicated on the idea that everyone can read and understand excellent literature–literature that has the capacity to engage the whole person, the imagination as well as the intellect" (*http:// www.greatbooks.org/printer/programs/junior/philosophy/sharing.shtml*).

The junior school series begins with kindergarten and goes through 9th grade (there is a high school series as well). The stories selected are an eclectic mix of well known "children's classics, folk tales and fairy tales, poetry, and modern short stories from cultures around the world" (*http:// www.greatbooks.org/printer/programs/junior/about/index.shtml*). The teacher is apparently required to take it on faith that the literature selected is worthy of the designation "great" and excellent. And Will does have faith that the JGB literature is better than that in basal readers.

The underlying pedagogical philosophy of the Junior Great Book Series is termed "shared inquiry." It is described as

a distinctive method of learning in which participants search for answers to fundamental questions raised by a text. This search is inherently active; it involves taking what the author has given us and trying to grasp its full meaning, to interpret or reach an understanding of the text in light of our experience and using sound reasoning. (ibid)

The program informs a teacher that "as a Shared Inquiry Leader, you do not impart information or present your own opinions, but guide participants in reaching their own interpretations. You do this by posing thought-provoking questions and by following up purposefully on what participants say." And this admonition ends with:

> In Shared Inquiry, participants learn to give full consideration to the ideas of others, to weigh the merits of opposing arguments, and to modify their initial opinions as the evidence demands...the Shared Inquiry method promotes thoughtful dialogue and open debate, preparing its participants to become able, responsible citizens, as well as enthusiastic, lifelong readers (*http://www.greatbooks.org/junior/philosophy/sharing.html*).

It is worth quoting this JGB stated philosophy at length to show how it squares with Will's working pedagogical philosophy of learning to think and why this program appealed to him when he first encountered it. Moreover, not only does this program, appeal to Will because it is supposedly "inherently active" in its "search for answers" in a text, it is the "shared," dialogic process, that implies, for Will, a conversation with students and with students across grade levels that represents "thinking."

Gaston

This is a story from the sixth level of Junior Great Books. Though it is labeled as a 6th grade story, therefore loosely understood as "Scott and Nate's story," Will determined that *Gaston* was a story that was appropriate for 6th, 7th and 8th grade, and he included the 4th graders Penny and Dylan in it. The students seemed nearly indifferent to whom the story "belonged." Though only Nate and Scott had the books, Will photocopied the story for the others (he usually destroyed the copies when he was finished, concerned about copyright issues). He wanted everyone to read the story. Dylan lost his copy and had to read along with Penny. Scott had left his book at home. The instructional conversation around *Gaston* took place in one day, in two sessions, the first in mid-morning for 43 minutes, the other after lunch for 31 minutes. I remember this day vividly because it was the day that I helped the students make apple cider.[9]

The general process of the shared inquiry, as Will has adapted it, involves asking the students to read, or have read to them, the story the evening before. Will assumes that he cannot rely on the initial reading happening at home, but encourages it all the same. The following day, the day of the first instructional conversation, begins with Will reading aloud the entire story while as many students as possible follow the written text. Often, prior to reading, Will poses a question, like that below for *Gaston*, that is suggested in the JGB teacher guide or one that Will creates. Sometimes for the younger students—Marlon, Mary, and Anna—Will has Nora and Danielle read the stories to them before his reading,

Before Will reads aloud *Gaston*, he poses to the students the question and writes on the board: "What makes a home?" He says this in a most provocative tone that students register as not having a self-evident answer (as Nate has said to me, "It's like he's saying, 'So you think you know, but not so fast buddy!'"). He wrote student responses on the board:

A place you can put things you need.
A place you sleep.
A place you relax.
A place you watch TV.
A place where your room is.
A place where you have things you like around you.

Will then proceeded to read the story aloud. He asked Marlon and Mary to listen in, and Anna if she wanted to listen while she colored and read her own book. He reads it straight through, without pausing to ask questions or make comments. After reading the story aloud, which took about 10 minutes, Will initiates their conversation by posing a question, not the one he put on the board (which he did not follow up on). Will took this question from the teacher's guide, which offers cues for the teacher, suggesting "fundamental questions posed by the text." Part of the design of Shared Inquiry is from the teacher to refrain from posing questions with simple answers.

The story *Gaston* is by the American-Armenian author William Saroyan, written in 1962. It is a complex and nuanced short story about a young girl who is visiting her father in Paris and is told from her point of view. The girl lives with her mother in New York. The child and father barely know each other. The story involves a conversation around an insect who crawls out of a peach pit on their kitchen table while they are having a snack. The father calls the bug "Gaston," a "boulevardier" (a bourgeoisie dandy who strolls the Parisian boulevards), who has lost his home and is now confused. The father succeeds in enticing the girl to see the bug having human qualities and who is now homeless. Within and through their conversation, they are so taken with Gaston that they look for more insects in the other peaches. When there are none to be found the father dashes out to market to find a "bad peach." When he returns, he finds out that the girl's mother has called, and that she is to be picked up by a chauffeur shortly and taken to her mother. When the girl tells the mother about Gaston, she is told not to be so silly. She then squashes the bug. Just as the father and girl start to emotionally connect, via their conversation around the bug, the mother intervenes and the girl kills the bug as surely as the conversation has been killed and they are strangers again. Their conversation is, in effect, a metaphor for their relationship. It is, by turns, stressed, fragile, elated, intriguing, trying to come to something through an object like an insect, and is then crushed and the girl leaves. All said, *Gaston* is not a straightforward tale; even the plot is obscure with an uneasy, if unhappy, ending.

Gaston Talk

Will pauses after he completes reading the text and begins the class conversation. The following extended transcript (over 2900 words) took approximately 28 minutes. Words presented in italics represent the speaker's verbatim reading of the story text. While this conversation takes place, Will notes student responses on a yellow legal pad.

> Teacher Will: When I read the story I said, ah, *"They were eating peaches as planned after a nap and now she sat across from a man who would have been a total stranger except that he was in fact her father."* Why did it say he was a stranger?
>
> Penny: Because she...
>
> TW: Okay, Penny.
>
> Penny: ...because she's never really like, um, seen him for long time.
>
> TW: Nor? [Will's nickname for Nora]
>
> Nora: Because her parents are like divorced or something and they don't live together so they don't get to see each other as much.
>
> TW: How do you think the girl feels about the way her father looks? About the way he dresses? Specifically the way he dresses.
>
> Nora: He dresses like, not really, not the same as her. Not like really fancy, but he's just wearing casual clothes. [long pause]
>
> TW: Do you think that ah, people she comes in contact with dress like this? Do you think...
>
> Penny: Not really?
>
> TW: Do you think she's around people who dress like this all of the time?
>
> Danielle: Um, no.
>
> TW: No? Why do you say that Danielle?

Danielle: If she was, then they wouldn't say anything about it. It wouldn't be needed.

Penny: It's just her dad. She thought her dad would be [inaudible]

TW: It was her dad and her dad, what?

Penny: She would think that her dad dresses the same as her.

TW: She thinks her dad should dress the same way as her and the people around her?

Penny: Yeah.

[pause]

TW: In the first part of this story, up to the part, after they get the peaches, okay, they find Gaston. Do you think the girl is comfortable or not comfortable in this, in his ah, home?

Scott: Um, not comfortable.

TW: Now you think she's not comfortable. What do you think Scott? Do you think she's, it never says this girl's name, so we don't know if it is Sally or Betty or what, but do you think the girl is comfortable here, when we're talking at the beginning of the story and you don't think she's comfortable.

[Scott pulls Nate's book. Nate leers at Scott as he does this and looks at Will as if to ask "What is he doing?"]

TW: 'Cause you have the book, Scott doesn't have the book, but Scott doesn't think she's comfortable. What do you think Nate? Do you think she's comfortable or not comfortable in this story? You think she's not comfortable?

Nate: Yeah, because she's not used to [inaudible]

TW: She's not comfortable because she's not used to what, I'm sorry?

Nate: She's not comfortable because she hasn't been around with the people dressed in different clothes.

TW: She's not comfortable because her father doesn't dress like the people she's used to being around, is that what you're saying?

Nate: Um-huh. Because probably in New York they all wear tie-dyed t-shirts and that.

TW: In where?

Nate: New York.

TW: Meester [Will's term of endearment for Marlon], what do you think, is she comfortable or is she not comfortable?

Marlon: She's not comfortable.

TW: She's not? This is interesting. Mary, what do you think, do you think she's comfortable in this setting?

Mary: [nods her head negatively]

TW: No, no one thinks she's comfortable? Danielle, what do you think? You thought she was comfortable didn't you?

Danielle: Uh.

TW: Kind of?

Danielle: Not comfortable enough to want to stay there, that she always wants to stay at her mother's.

TW: Like long enough to stay, but not forever?

Danielle: Yeah.

TW: Well, I'm going to get through this and then I'll come back to you and you can give me more on that. Penny what do you think, is she comfortable?

Nora: Sort of.

TW: Sort of [pausing to take notes]. How about you Dylan? What do you think?

Dylan: She's not comfortable.

TW: Not comfortable. Now, you know what's coming.

Multiple: hehehe Why?!

TW: Why! Me. Okay, I'll just go backwards. Danielle, show me, you thought she was kind of comfortable. Show me something in the book that there is evidence that she is not comfortable, in your opinion. Dylan, why did you say she's not comfortable?

Dylan: Because she thinks that her dad is a stranger.

TW: Does she think that her father is a stranger?

Scott: Sort of.

[Scott looking at the pages in Nate's book]

TW: Does she feel like he's a stranger? She's not comfortable because she thinks her father is a stranger [mimicking the words he's writing down]. Penny why do you think she's uncomfortable?

Penny: I think she's sort of comfortable.

TW: Sort of comfortable. Sort of not comfortable.

Penny: Because she sort of wants to stay with him. She doesn't really want to stay with him because she is at her home a lot. So, she kind of is comfortable because she's at her fathers and...

TW: There's something I want to pick up on. She is sort of comfortable. Say it one more time.

Penny: She sort of isn't comfortable because she really hasn't seen him for a number of years, because her mom is divorced from the father and hasn't stayed there before.

TW: Interesting. Nor, what else did you find, for being not comfortable?

Nora: Not comfortable?

TW: You said she's uncomfortable, not comfortable because her dad doesn't dress like her.

Nora: It was a different home.

TW: Because it was a different home?

Nora: Well it says on page 200 that *"It's nice but it's a lot different from our home."*

TW: Whoa, okay, let me get to page 200. Okay.

Nora: It's in the middle.

TW: *"It's nice,"* it's in the middle, *"It's nice but it's a lot different from our home,"* and that's the girl. Oh. [talking to Anna about her worksheet, who has approached him to show him something] I suppose it is. Okay, so if you start here with this passage, *"It's nice, but it's a lot different from our home,"* that's the girl talking about the difference in her father's home in Paris and her home in New York. And her father says, *"Yes, I suppose it is.* The girl says, *"It's like, it's kind of like Gaston's home."* Mmmmmmmmmm. *"...I squashed him. Why? Everybody squashes bugs...peach."* Let me get Danielle and then I'll come back to this. What'd you say Danielle?

Danielle: Well, on page 198...

TW: One ninety-eight, this is evidence that...

Danielle: On the top.

TW: Okay.

Danielle: It says, um, like she's talking about, okay, back on 197 it says that she says *"If the phone rings, well if it was my mother, what should I say? And then and everything and then if she wants me to go back, what should I say? Say yes if you want to go back. Do you want me to? Of course not, but the important thing is to do what you want and not what I want. "Why is that important?" Because I want you to be where you want to be. "I want to be here."*

TW: Ooh! So, I guess if you want to be someplace then you're comfortable with it? Would you want to be someplace you're not comfortable? I mean, you might have to be in a place where you're not comfortable, but if you had the choice, would you go to a place that you're not comfortable Nate? Where is a place that makes you uncomfort-able? The dentist maybe?

Nate: Well, sometimes I think I'm uncomfortable here because my mom kind of treats me a little bad.

Nora: What did he say?

TW: Is this your home though? Is this home? This isn't home, is it?

Nate: Sort of.

TW: Hmm. This is sort of your home? Um why do you think the father says, with what Danielle was saying, why does the father say, when they're talking on the phone, *"Tell her I've gone to get you a bad peach and anything else you want to tell her."* Why do you think the father says that to the girl? He's leaving. You know, if mom calls what should I say? Tell her I've gone to get you a peach, tell her what-ever you want. Why does he say that? [Nora waving her hand] Nor what do you think?

Nora: Because he wants her to be able to be like happy and know that she can say, she can do, like she can make her own decisions like what she wants to say instead of hav-ing people go, "Oh, you should wear that, oh you should do this."

Danielle: Okay, she wants to hear her say that she wants to stay there.

TW: [pauses to write] Um, do you think, do you think the mother would talk to the girl this way?

Nora: Probably not. That's just not...

TW: Say what she said again Nor about why the father said that he wanted her to be comfortable and make her own decisions.

Nora: Yeah.

TW: Do you think the mother would like her to make her own decisions?

Scott: No.

TW: No?

Scott: No.

TW: I wish you had a book because I would ask you immedi-ately to go find something. Who agrees with Scott?

Multiple: I do! I do!

TW: You two do, okay. Dylan agrees with Scott, but there again Dylan, I don't have a book for you either bud. Who agrees with Scott, that the mother would not let her make her own decisions?

Nora: Scott

 TW: Okay, if one person with a book does, please find evidence of that.

Dylan: I agree.

 TW: You agree? Why do you agree Dylan? While they're looking for evidence, what do you think?

  C: Well.

 TW: Do you agree that the mother would not let her daughter make her own decisions?

  C: Yes.

 TW: You agree that she would not let her. Why do you say that?

  C: Because she um, because she um, because she thinks that she's not old enough to do it yet.

Nora: Ooh!

 TW: Whoa, all these people, okay, okay. Danielle or Nor. You both have the same text. Danielle, what do you have and then I'll listen to what Nor has.

Danielle: Okay, like her mom calls and says...

 TW: What page?

Danielle: Um, page 198. Alright, I'm like, her mom calls and says that she's sending, she didn't ask her, she said *"I'm sending you a shock, a chef, chauffeur.* What's that word?

 TW: Chau-ffeur.

Danielle: Chauffeur. Okay to pick her up because there was a little party for someone's daughter who was also six and then tomorrow they would fly back to New York. She didn't say, she didn't ask, she just said that you have to come home so you can go to a party and you have to stay there.

 TW: She didn't say a thing though?

Nora: I'm on page 199!

 TW: Page 199.

Nora: In the middle!

 TW: In the middle.

Nora: The girl says *"and we'll have to squash it?"* And the mother replies, *"That's right."* The daughter is like, um saying "we'll have to squash it." Right, am I correct? Am I...?

 TW: She asks a question.

Nora: Yeah, I know.

 TW: *"And we'll have to squash it?"* It's a question rather than a statement.

Nora: I know but...

TW: So she's asking the question, she's asking her mother what to do, isn't she? And her mother says...

Nora: *"That's right."*

TW: Does she go on after "that's right, ah because dear, you can't play with bugs, they might have diseases, or they're dirty"?

Nora: No.

TW: She just ends up kind of cutting her off, doesn't she?

Nora: Um-huh.

TW: Any other places where you can see that the daughter isn't really allowed to make up her mind? Danielle?

Danielle: Well, because she wants to stay at her dad's house.

TW: O, Oh, she does?

Danielle: Yeah she does.

TW: Just a second. [writing down her response]

Danielle: If you look at page 200, second paragraph.

Danielle: His daughter was in her room in her best dress. *"My mother called, she said, "Chauffeur for me to go to another party." "Another?" "There's always a lot of them." "Will the chauffeur bring you back?" "No." "I like being at your house."*

Danielle: She likes being at her house, she wants to stay there, but she can't stay there because her mother already made the decision for her. And she, she doesn't, and that's why she's always, when she's talking to her dad it seems like she's saying, um, she's asking his opinion so she can do what he wants her to. Like, when she says, if she wants me to go back, what should I say? And he's, an he's giving her the choice where her mother wouldn't, because he would just say "No you can't go back because you're staying here." Because that the mother already made the choice and that's the end of it.

Penny: She's gotten so used to it that she just kind of does it.

TW: Um, as far as her making her own decisions, okay...I'll try to just kind of move this along, do you see any connection at all, between Gaston and the man?

Danielle: Yeah. He was lonely and so was the man.

TW: Gaston was lonely? Why was Gaston lonely?

Danielle: Because the they ruined his house.

TW: Because why?

Danielle: They ruined his house.

TW: They ruined his house.

Nora: And now he doesn't feel so secure because used to have like a whole peach around him and seed around him and now he's like open and in the wild and there's like...

Danielle: But, the guy's, the father's home was having his daughter there.

TW: So are you saying that the father doesn't have a home anymore?

Danielle: Um, what I'm saying is that it doesn't feel like home, because home to him is where is family is. Because he loves his daughter.

TW: Nor?

Nora: Oh, what?

TW: I thought you had your hand up.

Nora: No.

TW: Oh, I mistook this for raising your hand, I'm sorry. Scott, do you see any connection between the man and Gaston?

Scott: Yeah

TW: And?

R: They both...they're both lonely.

TW: They're both lonely. Penny?

Penny: They both don't have anybody to live with. Like, you have to have people, have somebody to live with.

TW: Do people always, do you have to have, do you have to live with someone to have a home or a house?

?: No.

TW: Can you live alone and be happy?

Nate: You could, if you're surrounded by the things that you like.

Danielle: It was, he was fine until her daughter came, and when his daughter came...

TW: Was he fine?

Danielle: He was alright.

TW: Was he fine before his daughter came?

Nora: I don't know, it doesn't say here in the book.

TW: Well, what do you think?

Danielle: No.

TW: What do you think happened to get him from where he was to where he is? They got divorced. We've already established that.

Danielle: An she said...

TW: What could be a reason maybe that the parents are divorced?

Danielle: Probably because they don't like each other. I don't know.

C: They fighted a lot.

TW: Well, find something in the story that would give you some evidence.

Scott: I know.

TW: Scott.

R: Because when he says, maybe, um, the father wants, um, the kid to make her own decisions and the mother just wants to give orders.

Nora: I know where it says evidence.

TW: Nor.

Nora: When she, when the girl's on the phone with the mother. Um on page 199 in the middle, the mother asks, *"Is he crazy?* And the daughter replies yes. I mean no, and it goes on. But, they like can't get along because he's like, like studying, like nature, like why does this happen? Why the bug doesn't have a home anymore, oh no what are we going to do? And the wife's more like the business person, like the stock has gone up like a lot. Get it?

TW: Sometimes.

Multiple: Hehehehehehehehe

Danielle: Um he was like really happy that she was there and um, cause he hadn't seen them for a long time and he was probably kind of disappointed because obviously her mother got to take custody of her.

TW: Nat what did you want to say?

Nora: I wanted to say that her mom's like wants her to get over it.

TW: Get over what?

Nora: Like squashing bugs.

TW: Oh, the bug, okay, I see what you're saying.

Nora: And the dad's like "oh no."

TW: Do these sound like two different people to you?

?: Um-huh.

TW: How would you characterize the woman?

Nora: Um, business person.

Nora: Business person. Business person.

Nora: Rich.

TW: Rich? Okay, where's Nora here? [looking at his notes and writing down her comment] Nor, rich, business person.

Nora: Well because I mean if they have like a chauf.

TW: A chauffeur. How would you characterize the father?

?: Um, more…

Nora: Simple! He's simple because it said in the story they went down three, three staircases

TW: Three flights of stairs?

Nora: Yeah, three flights of stairs, that's what I meant to say.

TW: And this would…?

Nora: So he's got, he either lives in like an apartment or like he has a really big house.

TW: Well, it's called a walk-in apartment. I used to live in one. And when there's no elevator it means that it's not a fancy building to live in. You have to walk up and down every time. So I, so I think you're right. Okay, for right now, we'll come back to Gaston later. Okay. Um, recess. Recess to 10:00. Outside to play. Have fun. Anna wake up, it's daytime here. Is she asleep?

S: Okay for right now. We'll come back to Gaston. Recess.

Multiple: Woo hoo.

This conversation continued that afternoon, after lunch, for another 31 minutes and proceeded in similar fashion with Will seeking involvement of as many students as possible, using questions provided by the JGB teachers guide for questions and ideas from their conversations about the relationship between the father and the girl and how they imagine the bug Gaston as having human traits. The second session seemed rushed, and the school day ended minutes after this second conversation ended. I noted that Will did not assign any assignments or writing after this second conversation, such as end of the story comprehension questions. The story unit had ended that afternoon.

When I asked students about this story their responses ranged from "interesting" to "boring." Danielle said that she thought the story was intriguing, "for a sixth grade story." Nate said he found it kind of interesting that the girl did not want to stay with her father. When I asked him what he meant about him saying he is uncomfortable at his house, he said it's because his mother disciplines him harshly, and that, like the girl, he could not make decisions. Nora said it was "a sad story because the parents don't get along and are divorced and the kid was a rich brat." Danielle felt that kids need to be nice to their parents, and vice verse. Penny says she thought the girls' mother had no respect for the girl's father and that they should "have a chance to love each other." Dylan, indicated that they should not be eating fruit with bugs and that it must be nice to be driven by a chauffeur. Both Mary and Marlon said they were bored, especially Marlon, but Mary, I noted, listened keenly to the story and the conversation and said she thought the girl ought not to have squashed the bug because that was not nice. It seemed from the transcript and my conversation with them later, that nearly all the students were attending to this sixth grade story in the morning and afternoon.

Taken as a representative of the corpus of the transcript of the instructional conversation, it is possible to detect in this excerpt from the time spent on *Gaston* Will's learning to take on the JGB as part of his teaching. We see him in fits and starts, especially at the outset, writing down student responses, not directly following up on some of their responses. It is evident in the transcript that Will does more of the talking than the students. He takes more turns at talk than the students and his turns at talk are longer, which seems to rub against the JGB facilitator's guide which states that he "guide" students in their own interpretations. As he says, "Sometimes you can't help yourself and when you don't get a response or enough of a response, you just jump in and talk. I know the goal is to get them to talk, but I'm also in charge [laughs]." Will is expressing an insight into his own dilemma. Though he has all sorts of social control at the school, in order to have something resembling a conversation, he cannot control the students' responses. Conversation is, by definition, contingent and unpredictable; controlling an interlocutor's response makes the interaction something other than a conversation. "All you can do," Will reflects, "is work with what they give you and hopefully you can have a meeting of the minds, at some point. I still cannot give them the answers. That, so they say, is what the [Junior] Great Books [program] is about, I guess. It could have gone smoother." When I asked him further what he meant by that, he said that it was a challenge to keep track of all the students' responses, writing them down, and deciding what to do with them once he had them. He says he needs to make some judgments about what is a generative response so as to move the conversation forward while not excluding some students' comments. Will faces a genuine, and classic, teaching tension indeed.

But we also see Will trying to keep the conversation going, around some questions that do not have easy or yes/no answers. We also see the students joking that Will is going to ask "why" and not devolving into a conventional pattern evaluative questions (looking for right answers about discrete bits of the story). Will also noted that Danielle and Nora were offering some of the more sophisticated responses, when it was Scott and Nate's story. "But that's okay," he said, "because they are modeling for them how to deal with a story." When I ask if there was any benefit to reading this particular story, he replied that "It's not straightforward. It's a sad story, really, and I suppose it helps them think about home and their families." The educative value, for Will, comes from their capacity and opportunity to engage in an extended conversation about a story. And being able to take part in such a conversation represent for him evidence of student engagement and learning; it is for Will a kind of intellectual performance (though he does not use that language) that objectifies for him intellectual engagement. It expresses some learning or "thinking."

The excerpt of the *Gaston* conversation is relatively early in the school year. It is fair to say that Will's teaching of JGB became more refined as the school year progressed. I now turn to the second excerpt JGB, a discussion of *Wisdom's Wages and Folly's Pay* that takes place a few months later in February, 2000.

Wisdom's Wages and Folly's Pay

This book is part of the level 4 (4th grade) series. Written by Howard Pyle and published in 1895 from his book *Twilight Land*, the story takes place somewhere in Old World Europe and concerns the relationship and travels of two neighbors, one a wise man, who is a doctor and a magician, the other the "simpleton of simpletons." The wise man, Simon Agricola, asks the simpleton, Babo, if he would like to be his companion traveling the countryside and making their fortune through performing feats of benevolent magic. Babo agrees. Simon Agricola eventually tires of Babo's bumbling and thwarting of potential fortunes and he angrily dispatches Babo with the admonishment, "Think well! Think Well! Before you do what it is you are about to do, think well!" (p. 131). Later, Babo says this out loud to himself, unaware that nearby are some nervous thieves with a pot of stolen money. Thinking that Babo is an agent of the king, the thieves get scared, drop the stolen loot and flee. Babo becomes a hero and is rewarded by the king. In the end Babo gets rich and Simon Agricola, the wise man, stays poor.

Wisdom's Wages and Folly's Pay Talk.

Following JGB procedure, the students were to have read, or to have read to them, the story the day or night before. Then in the same class, from which the following excerpts are taken, Will reads aloud the story, as he did with *Gaston*. Teacher Will asks the students to pay attention as he reads the story and to take notes on where in the text they felt "someone was being smart or being stupid." The excerpts (over 850 words) below amount to approximately thirteen minutes of talk. Again, text is italics represent verbatim quoting of the JGB text.

> Teacher Will: This was Penny's story and Dylan's story so let's start with them, okay. Penny, where is a place you marked?
>
> Penny: I marked on [flipping pages] on a hundred and thirty-one.
>
> TW: One hundred and thirty-one. Who's being, oh, is somebody being smart or stupid?

Penny: Babo.

TW: Babo? Is he being smart or stupid?

Penny: Smart.

TW: Okay.

Penny: It's about the last paragraph.

TW: Last paragraph.

Penny: [quoting from the text] *When the two thieves heard Babo's piece of advice they thought that the judges officers were after then for sure. And so they dropped the pot of money and away they scampered as fast as they could.*

TW: How is that evidence of Babo being smart?

Penny: He's being smart because he says advice to the, um, the um, the thieves so they would drop the money and they would not steal it.

TW: Why did he say what he said? Why did Babo say, *Think, think well, think before you do what you're about to do, think well.* Why did he say that? Did he give them advice? He's giving them advice, Nate?

Nate: No.

TW: Why not, what do you mean?

Dylan: No, because he had voices that woke him up and he thought, "where would it be?" so he said the advice that the doctor had gave him.

TW: Oh, so you don't think that he, you think that this is just the first thing that popped into his head?

Nate: Um-huh.

TW: Do you have any evidence of that?

Nate: Well, when he just woke up…

TW: Where does it say that in the story? Where does it say that? Where's your evidence?

Dylan: Teacher Will, I have one.

Scott: I know where. I know where. I know where. Um, um, where like

Nate: *They squabbled and bickered and angry till the noise till they made woke Babo, and he sat up. Then the first thing he thought was the advice the doctor had gave him the evening before.*

TW: Oh. So, Penny, what do you have to say?

Penny: Like Nate.

TW: Well, I mean, do you see where Nate's coming from with this?

Penny: Yes.

TW: Do, has it changed your mind at all? Or do you still think that this was, was an example of Babo being smart?

Penny: Well.

TW: Or do you think it was Babo consciously being smart or that it was just the first thing that popped into his head and he said it?

Nora: I have that spot marked too.

TW: Oh, you all have it? Okay, so for everybody, I guess my question is, do you agree with Nate?

Dylan: I don't.

TW: Now, Penny, you thought it was an example of being smart and Nate disagreed with you.

Nate: No, I said it was something smart too.

TW: Oh, you think that's an example of Babo being smart?

Nate: Yeah.

TW: Nor, what do you think?

Nora: I say smart, because sometimes things don't just pop into your mind, you have to think about it. I mean, like if we were to be discussing the matter on how deep the Indian Ocean was, somebody would say, um, "I had waffles for breakfast this morning." You wouldn't just say that.

TW: Well, no, I see where you guys are coming from. I see your point. So you all think it's an example of Babo being smart? Okay? If you look up at the top of the page, on page 131. *"Here it is," said Simon Agricola, "Think well. Think well. Before you do what you are about to do, think well."* Do you think that that is an example of, Simon Agricola being smart?

Multiple: Um-huh.

Nora: Yes.

TW: In what way? Why is that an example of Simon Agricola being smart?

Nora: He's giving advice because...

TW: He's giving advice, but was it good advice?

Nora/Scott: Yes.

TW: Simon Agricola is giving Babo good advice? Is that what you're saying?

Multiple: Um-huh.

Dylan: Yeah, because he, um, he didn't go to the thieves, that's why. So then, um, then he, then Babo was walking around with the money and then the king's guard and he, um, told it to the king and then the king asked for his advice and then, um, the next day he paid for it.

Scott: But, um, if, um, Babo was the first one to think of the, um, um, the advice, um, he, he, so like if Agricola was in

Babo's place, um, then he would have thought the advice and um, um…

TW: Did you lose your train of thought a little bit Scott?

[This bit of discourse took about ten minutes and continues for another five minutes or so beyond the end of the excerpt here. Will then moves to involve the second grader, Mary, who is vigorously waving her hand.]

TW: Mary! You found something?

Mary: Uh-huh. [Page] One hundred and twenty. *"Then I will show you," said Babo. He…*

Nora: [whispers] spread

Mary: *…spread the bed of*

Nora: [whispers] of cold

Mary: *…of cold, dead…*

Scott: [whispers] ashes

Mary: *…ashes upon his…*

Scott: [whispers] palm

Mary: *…palm. "Now," said he, "I will take the umber…*

Nora/Scott [whispers] ember

Mary: *…ember upon that."*

TW: Is that an example of something of Babo being smart or stupid?

Mary: Being smart.

TW: Being smart, okay.

Scott: Being smart because, um, he's taking the dry ashes to make sure he doesn't get burned by the coals.

Nate: Actually…

TW: What Nate, I'm sorry, what?

Nate: Actually the ashes burnt him.

TW: I don't know.

Nora: You can't set fire to ashes on ashes.

The discussion of whether and how ashes are hot and can therefore burn someone goes on for another 7 minutes, at Will's behest because, as he told me, he did not want to them to stop. This entire conversation (including Will's oral reading of the text) took over 50 minutes. This conversation on *Wisdom* continued the following day for just under an hour and the day after that for another 50 minutes.

In these excerpts we can see Will maneuvering to encourage students to offer interpretation. He also consistently presses for them to find evidence in the text to support their interpretations, especially in *Wisdom*, not merely their "feelings" or their "reader's response." There is disagreement among the students, and some indication that they can hold that someone can be both smart and stupid, depending on one's point of view (an important aspect of modern literature, especially understanding the modern novel). Moreover, this conversation substantially involves two 4th graders (Dylan and Penny), a 5th grader (Nate), a 6th grader (Scott), and a 7th grader (Nora). The 2nd graders, Mary and Marlon, are listening in, Mary actively participates in one stretch (with her siblings helping her out), and Anna floats in and out of attention while she colors. In other words, practically all the students are involved in this conversation.

Nonplussed by my question about the value of reading and talking about stories and about *Wisdom* specifically, the students see this interaction as part of doing school here. When I ask about the discussion of the story, each student (save Anna and Danny) respond without hesitation. "I still think Babo is the stupid one," Nate tells me. "He simply repeated the words he heard. He's dumb and just lucky!" Scott said he thought that Simon Agricola should have been more patient, then "they both would have gotten the money, maybe." Nora indicates she felt there was something that got missed altogether, that "even when you are smart, like a professor or whatever he was [Simon], that you can still be poor." They are still thinking about the story and answer my question immediately. The speed of their responses would seem to say something about the effect these stories and the conversation are having: they are becoming accustomed to engaging in talk about books and some sophisticated literature. Even Mary says "It's real easy to talk about the books. It's fun." When I ask what is easy, she notes that "Will just wants us to talk." And when I asked if she was afraid of being wrong in her answers, she said, "Not a lot. It's not like spelling when you get a word wrong you, they're wrong."

GREAT BOOKS AT UPPER RILL
AS BUDDING AUTHENIC PEDAGOGY

These extended excerpts give some indication of the contingent give and take of Will's conversation-based model of instruction in JGB. In the world of elementary school academic conversations, this kind of sustained "talk about text," evident both in both *Gaston* and especially *Wisdom*, within and across school days and involving children across several grade levels, is rather remarkable (see Raphael, Gavelek, & Daniels, 1998; Gavelek & Raphael, 1996). This is a departure from conventional classroom discourse, which is characterized by getting students to correctly answer factual questions posed by the teacher (and in things like worksheets), not the literary text (see Florio-Ruane & Raphael, 2001). This is itself part of a larger pattern of conventional classroom instructional interaction that Mehan (1979) describes as being structured by evaluative communication as a teacher searches for correct answers ("Yes, that's right" or "No, that's incorrect"). These excerpts of classroom discourse reveal a good deal of pedagogical complexity. *Gaston* entails some emotional complexity of a strained and fragile relationship that is not easily explained and getting students to discuss this without *telling* them what the story is about and how its parts fit together. *Wisdom's Wages and Folly's Pay* does not simplistically yield the answer to the question of whether Babo was smart or stupid. Each story has a particular irony. In *Gaston*, a young girl and her father can be strangers; in *Wisdom*, a simpleton can mindlessly say out loud to himself the intelligent advice of a wise man made him rich. While ironies can certainly be explained directly to students, the shared inquiry urges teachers' restraint from telling and explanation, making the pedagogical task all the more challenging. Will could simply point out the irony for them, but his would undermined the Great Books goals and, in effect, contradict some Will's own professed teaching values.

What is further noteworthy here is that, broadly speaking, this conversation-based pedagogy is not explicitly teacher-centered or textbook-centered. To be sure, Will plays an important and forceful mediating role, but this is not a teacher-dominated conversation that is convergent, i.e., getting students to simple, correct answers. To be sure, this conversation is focused on the text, but students' responses and interpretations are weighed heavily in the course of the interaction. The text does not yield simple answers of whether and how Babo and/or Simon Agricola are smart or stupid, that is if one takes the story as a complicated piece of literature. The particular irony built into *Wisdom's Wages and Folly's Pay* requires a reader needs to take on multiple perspectives to understand stupidity in the context of the story. Instead of using literature to preach to children—e.g., about being good, honest, and hard working, listening to authorities, the need to make friends, getting along—whatever lesson is built into *Wisdom's Wages and Folly's Pay* to edify the reader comes through an oblique situation and the moral and social dilemmas into which the story's characters are thrown

This kind of pedagogy resembles "authentic" literary conversation found, for instance, in a university English seminar and echoes the kind of ambitious instruction literacy reformers argue for (e.g., Florio-Ruane et al., 2001). What is notable is that kind of student- and conversation-based pedagogy does not flow from any imposed policy in or around Upper Rill. It emerges from Will's own sense of what he thinks is important and what he thinks schooling should be about, i.e., learning to think. He has the opportunity *and* the means to carry this out in his one-teacher setting and by the autonomy that he is afforded by Cal, who effectively buffers him from more constraining expectations. Cal requires Will to be neither highly specific about individual students' progress through their respective grade-level curricula nor that he engage in a constant assessment. Such expectation would effectively thwart Will's capacity to carry out teaching with and from JGB.

It is worth noting that Will takes on very little "formal" assessment with the JGB units (e.g., quizzes), though he has begun to incorporate student writing responses. He does have students sometimes complete "comprehension" questions that appear in both his teacher guide and the student books. But his primary way of "assessing" whether the students are learning comes from the conversation themselves and the notes he takes during them. For Will, the main advantage comes from the students capacity to engage in sustained conversation, which for Will is evidence that students are "thinking." As such, this pedagogy has what I term properties of progressive properties whose emergence I take up at greater length in the next chapter.

NOTES

1. Metropolitan Achievement Test, a standardized, norm referenced test used by the school.

2. Will does not speak of it in these terms precisely. The language is mine. When I went to verify this claim I am making, to check for discordance in understanding the extent of Cal's expectations and Will's autonomy, I posed this to Cal in almost this exact language. He said that this is "exactly" how it is from his point of view. In other words Cal and Will understand each other.

3. Will attended an in-service at the Educational Service Unit in the spring and was told by another Class One teacher that he should conform his social studies curriculum to all the other Class Ones in the county, so that they had a uniform social studies curriculum that could be aligned with the state standards and a common assessment device (e.g., test). This made Will irate, in part because he did not like this teacher—"an idiot at another school telling me what I had to do"– but more because it violated his strong sense of autonomy and the implied bargain with Cal, the only authority he feels he needs to respond to, and introduced a foreign expectation.

4. It has been pointed out to me (Helen Hazi, personal communication, 2001) that I may have been the first interested party, and a non-teacher, to ever really ask Will for his working philosophy and personal beliefs about teaching, and, more importantly, that he has never been asked to describe and connect his views to his practice. My original view that he is inarticulate may be misplaced. My guess is that Will is coping with the reputation his teacher education program had and that he did not want to simply parrot its published precepts and thereby sound, in his words, stupid.

5. The late Madeleine Hunter was an educational psychologist and instructional theorist who enjoyed great popularity in teacher education in the 1970s and 1980s. Her behaviorist methods are now widely discredited in educational scholarship, having been replaced by more "cognitive" or "con-

structivist" approaches to teaching and learning. However, her language of behavioral "outcomes" and "mastery learning" has a powerful residue throughout teacher education and school district policies, mostly due to its amenability to rational planning and standardized testing. Madeline Hunter is indeed still king in many ways.

6.   Acronym for Activities Integrating Math and Science, a National Science Foundation funded project. See http://www.aimsedu.org/Activities/index .html.

7.   A magic square is an arrangement of numbers in a matrix. The challenge is to arrange the numbers 1–9 using each number once. Each number occurs once in an arrangement so that the sum of the entries of any row, any column, or any main diagonal is the same. Here is the simplest of 3 x 3 matrix that Will has used:

> He feels that there is addition and some on-your-feet thinking needed for solving these kinds of problems and the students seem to enjoy them. And while it appears as something fun, both he and the students see this as part of their mathematics curriculum. The high point of this activity is when they work it out together, with Will writing on the board, a kind of "thinking with" the students rather than Will telling them the answer.

8.   This seems to be the intellectual cradle of the Great Books association.

9.   Schedule for that day:
   8:30   Magic Squares (math activity, grade level)
           Clean desks get ready for Great books
   8:50   Great Books, *Gaston*
   9:30   Recess
   10:15   Make Apple Cider
   11:30   Lunch/Recess
   1:00   Math (students work individually in their assignments. Will holds individual meetings with students at his desk on their assignments).
   2:00   Discussion with students as to whether making apple cider is any cheaper than buying it at the store. Will leads computations (how many gallons of cider in a bushel, how much a bushel costs, etc. Will has Scott call a local grocery store to get their price on apple cider)
   2:30   Music
   3:00   Great Books *Gaston*.
   3:30   Dismiss

CHAPTER 6

A CRITICAL COMPARISON
OF BIGHAND AND
UPPER RILL SCHOOLS

In Chapters 4 and 5 I examined ethnographically how curriculum and instruction are organized at Bighand and Upper Rill Schools. More specifically, it has been my effort to show how these cases of instruction, when taken on their own terms, are rendered sensible within their respective contexts. Bighand's modern recitation pedagogy is remarkably efficient, especially so when viewed against the local definitions of the purposes of schooling and the widespread expectations in which Mrs. Hoffman is embedded. There is a great deal of consonance between the pedagogy in the school and community expectations of what school is for. "Getting through" makes perfect sense there and Mrs. Hoffman's recitation system of "classes" is a remarkably effective, and efficient, device for fulfilling the expectations of ensuring that students "keep up" with their town school counterparts and that they "be ready" for middle and secondary school. Upper Rill's conversations are similarly sensible in that they emerge as a function of Will Tomlinson's self-imposed agitation that he needs "something better" in order to get his students "to think" and that he has the autonomy and an administrator's support to experiment.

What makes these schools' practices instructive is how radically different they are. Bighand and Upper Rill schools reside in very similar communi-

Naturally Small: Teaching and Learning in the Last of the One-Room Schools, pages 97–111
Copyright © 2004 by Information Age Publishing

ties, with deep roots in agriculture. Both are Class One, country schools and exist as a result of virtually identical historical circumstances. These schools are in the eastern half of the same state, more prairie than Plains, in communities originally settled by German farming immigrants. The students are, generally speaking, quite similar, all of them having some kind of connection to agriculture in their family histories in their respective communities. *All* the students at both schools, by the measures of standardized testing,[1] are performing satisfactorily at grade level and the parents of each school believe that their children are succeeding. *None* of parents I interviewed at either school believed their children were in any way "behind" academically and, consequently, have implicit or explicit faith in the academic accomplishment of the schools. Each school presents its teacher with a diversity of ages, up to grade 8. These settings present a unique pedagogical challenge for both Mrs. Hoffman and Teacher Will that is rarely seen in the graded, public school culture.

How is it, then, that under such similar circumstances and challenges that two teachers can develop such radically different forms of instruction? While this question can be answered in great part in how each teacher interprets their settings and the definitions of his/her work—each school really is a shadow of its teacher—it is also worth considering ethnographically and more deeply the functions of the organization of teaching in each school. Instead of simply comparing these schools, and their teacher's intentions and arrive at an early, naïve judgment—that somehow Bighand's instruction is better because of its efficiency or that Upper Rill's is superior because of its progressive-sounding commitment to conversation and thinking—or at some unsophisticated relativism—both schools are good in their own ways and forms of teaching in each lead to satisfactory test scores—it is worth considering what is obtained symbolically by the forms of teaching that occur in each school. While I present each school as having its own model *of* instruction, it is important to indicate that I hold neither as an ideal model *for* instruction.[1] Rather, what is potentially generative is how we can draw some inferences as to how the functions of teaching feed into, reinforce and sustain kinds of academic organization and teaching practices. In turn, this offers something to think with, to paraphrase Claude Levi-Strauss, about the place of small schools in educational reforms.

BIGHAND SCHOOL: CONSERVATIVE PEDAGOGY AND DEFENDING A WAY OF LIFE

As I have written elsewhere (Swidler, 2000), it is easy for reform-minded educators, urban and rural alike, to leap to criticism of Mrs. Hoffman and her practice. Her "classes" are intellectually conservative, almost completely textbook-bound, and teacher controlled. Student interest and intentionality are epiphenomenal pedagogical concerns. It is more than possible to claim that her teaching is not academically demanding and does not press students for "higher order thinking." The classes embody a concept of knowledge that it is created elsewhere by experts and codified in textbooks. This, in turn, implies a passive theory of student learning, i.e., students will simply learn what is presented to them in textbooks. This modern recitation-based teaching does not involve any "place-based curriculum" or "pedagogy of place" that many rural school reformers see as the inherent value of rural schools and, therefore, their chief resource for curriculum development (see Theobald & Nachtigal, 1995). Students completing written assignments and worksheets and scoring well in commercially produced tests and quizzes are taken as unproblematic proxies for learning. The language of curriculum development and reform of the last two decades, such as "constructivism," "cooperative grouping," "whole language," "authentic assessment," and "teaching for understanding," does not emerge in the talk of Mrs. Hoffman or her administrators, Stan Vogt and Jim Hauser. There are no sustained, common academic projects in which students of varying age levels engage. Academic work is composed entirely of discrete assignments in content areas that have no connection to one another; there are no interdisciplinary activities. And, Mrs. Hoffman's usage of "classes" can be viewed as expedient classroom management rather than a product of her professional reflection.

Any analysis of public schooling and teaching practices cannot avoid criticisms such as these, especially as reformers seek to link size to school effectiveness. In seeking to understand the coherence and sensibility of Mrs. Hoffman's practice, I find that there are important things to consider before leaping to a deficit critique. First, I believe this pedagogy is quite consonant with the conservative nature of teaching in public graded schools with centralized curricula, which is regularly well documented in research and reform literature (e.g., Cohen & Hill, 2001; Elmore, Peterson, & McCarthy, 1996). Conservative, textbook-centered instruction is hardly the exclusive possession of small country schools. We cannot blame this teacher for a country school pedagogy that is a very close cousin of graded school teaching. The traditions of conservative teaching generally would seem to play into Mrs. Hoffman's pedagogy (see Cohen, 1988; Cuban, 1996). More importantly, a culturally sensitive analysis would take into account the rural context of the school and it relationship to Mrs. Hoffman's practice and it to this that I now turn.

Community Values as Context of Bighand Pedagogy

The structure of instruction at Bighand School is infused with community values, including respect for and assent to adult authority (i.e., the teacher as manager and academic organizer), independence, hard work, following through, and self-discipline (i.e., completing one's work, no matter what one thinks of it). These values could be described as rural or agricultural, and they are frequently referred to as a "work ethic" by Bighand parents community members. These are almost always invoked when they speak of the virtue of one-room schooling in general and at Bighand in particular.

For instance, in the late fall of 1998, just after harvest, Mary and Deborah's father, Tom, described the differences between Bighand School and "town schools" this way:

> Well, I think the work ethic is different, especially in a rural school like this because you're in a farming community and you know, when you farm, you've got to enjoy the work because there is no money in it. The rewards are not financial. And I think the kids see this, and it helps them for a little bit better work ethic because it makes them realize that you have to do something to earn something. Now, all of the kids in this school do not come from farm families, but they see it.

And when reflecting upon the relationship between his children's experience at Bighand School, farm life and the work ethic of "following through" and "hard work," Tom avers:

> Well, I mean, they're living in it. They're living in the middle of it. They have come to accept the fact that there are tractors in the spring of the year and it's a very busy time and things are happening very quickly. And they come to realize during the fall, during the harvest season, that the combines are rolling, and you know, at ten, eleven, twelve o'clock at night. The guys across the road are combining. There are trucks on the road all of the time. They know it is another busy time of the year. They've come to realize that this is how they get paid. If they had two very critical times of the year and that sets the basis for their yearly wages. You got to get the crop in the ground and you've got to get it out. And I think that concept carries over to the school and she [Mrs. Hoffman] understands this.

It is not simply the case that Bighand School is "instilling" these values in students. For adult community members, the school board and parents the school does do that. But, from a culturally nuanced point of view, children's socialization into these values is intertwined with larger community and parental concerns that are not necessarily self-evident. These interpenetrating values include, in an ascending order of abstraction, secondary school success, a suspicion of youth culture, and symbolic defense of community and a way of life.

Secondary School Success

From my conversations and interviews with school board members, the administrators, and especially parents, what they say they want from school seems no different than what many want for their children, that school somehow "prepares them for life." But more immediately, they are concerned that the school prepare children to cope with life in large, graded middle and secondary schools in which their children will inevitably enroll, part of "being ready." Not only do parents and community members want this, they believe that it is happening. There is a pervasive lore in the Bighand community that graduates of the school do very well in secondary school. And like all lore, it is taken seriously by the folk who transmit it; it is not pure fiction to these people. The parents of high school students who have recently graduated from Bighand (like Deborah and Mary's sister) and those who have transferred to middle school (like Daisy's brother) regularly indicate that their children are not only "ready" but undeniably "ahead" when they enter high school or middle school. Molly's mother, a former Bighand board member, is probably the staunchest defender of the school in this regard. Her eldest son graduated from Surrey High School and is presently studying agricultural mechanics at a trade school, that she says has competitive admissions. She states plainly, "I cannot think of anything that could have prepared him [for high school] better than Mrs. Hoffman."

There is other empirical evidence for the Bighand community on student success. The county superintendent, Stan Vogt, informed me that Bighand students' scores for the Iowa Test of Basis Skills "are well above the median" for Class One schools in the county.[2] He proudly states that Bighand "students never become an academic problem" in the middle and high schools to which they transfer. The superintendent of Riverview Schools, himself a Class One school graduate, is effusive about the country schools who are affiliated with his district: "The kids from the one-room, Class One schools we get do an outstanding job. We have had no problems with kids from the Class Ones since I have been here." As the respected superintendent of the largest affiliated district, he has the clout to pressure the closing of Bighand, and Riverview would consequently absorb its property tax revenue and state aid. Though the superintendent of Sparta-Johnville Schools is understood in the Bighand community to be hostile to the school, he finds it hard to criticize the students from Bighand who enroll in his schools. He considers Bighand a revenue drain from his district and states vaguely that the students "have deficiencies when they first come." But when I ask him if the students ever fail or become discipline problems, he grudgingly admits that Bighand's graduates are successful high school students. And when I draw the conclusion for him that the Bighand students contribute positively to his schools, he responded tersely,

"You could say that. But at what cost? That's a lot of money for a small school and a small number of kids." This information and these sentiments about student success circulate thoroughly within the Bighand School community.[2]

Bighand parents and community members have strong, logical ideas about why one learns to be a good student at Bighand. The habits of self-discipline and following through on one's work learned at Bighand would seem to help one get through middle and secondary school and be a good student. In the large graded middle and secondary schools, students have little consistent and close contact with their teachers like they do in Bighand and this creates one of the bumpy points of transition for students. For instance, Mary and Deborah's big sister Kayla, a graduate of Bighand and now a sophomore at Riverview High School, indicated to me that the one of the hardest things in the transition to high school is the lack of regular personal contact with her teachers. She was perplexed about how she had to make appointments with the teachers, sometimes days in advance, about what were for her immediate concerns (e.g., how to complete a particular assignment). Yet, paradoxically, she was able to cope with this predicament precisely because she felt that she had learned to stick with her work and not give up in frustration. Her mother, Julie, describes how she sees the organization of Bighand School helping Kayla:

> At the school there is more than one grade that the teacher has to work with and so she can't just devote the attention to all of them on an assignment and make sure that they do it. [Students] do have to do some planning and organization and some self-management skills, which again is important when you get older. And, of course, they have to be more self-motivated to complete their work on their own. And they don't… well just from being in the public city schools, I know that isn't the way it is. The teacher really organizes your day for you…[Kayla] had to be responsible to get her work done and she had to organize what she was going to do and when. She did not get distracted.

This idea of a teacher organizing the day for students rubs several Bighand parents the wrong way since, for them, this undermines self-discipline, independence and responsibility, part of a work ethic and of "life values," as Julie puts it. Bighand's classes fit well with these values and help in their acquisition. To participate competently in the academic life in the school, a Bighand student is expected to keep up with the flow of the classes and this finds little room for resistance and requires some self-monitoring. Failure to do one's work or be ready for classes disrupts the flow of a highly organized pattern of academic life in this school and undermines, indirectly, community values.

Troublesome Youth Culture

A persistent theme running through my conversations and interviews with parents is their distrust of popular youth culture. This distrust seems to grow from a mixture of media images and personal knowledge of kids who have gotten into trouble in and out of school. One January evening I had dinner at a Riverview diner with the Bighand Neighborhood Club. This group is an informal descendent of the old agricultural extension women's club, now composed of the "young mothers" (those with school-age children and younger). Of the Bighand mothers, only Julie participates. The dominant topic of our conversation was their very real anxiety about the sexualized atmosphere of schools, in the way girls dress and what they sense to be increased sexual activity among younger girls. They told stories of young girls they know of getting into trouble and becoming pregnant. They lament what one mother called a "lack of basic values," what they perceive to be a skyrocketing teenage pregnancy rate, and a loss of control over their own children to a decadent MTV-inspired youth culture. When speaking of her children, a Bighand community mother, whose children option into Sparta-Johnville schools, puts it this way:

> We're worried that they will no longer listen to us but their peers and God knows what else they see on TV. It's scary at times. I wish we could just cut them off from it, for a while at least until they have enough sense to figure out what's right and what's wrong. But you cannot keep them locked up forever. It scares me to death what could happen.

Schooling at Bighand offers two things to parents who are concerned about this. For one, it offers separation from, and postponement of entry into, the youth culture they see as troublesome. More importantly, they view life at the school, which means life with recitations, as providing their children with a small scale schooling experience that helps them learn to get along with others and acquire the self-discipline to resist the youth culture and avoid, as Molly's mother says with elegant concision, "leaning toward trouble." That is, the orderly, quiet atmosphere of the school, required of a recitation-based curriculum, helps students acquire the self-discipline to cope with the pressures of the youth culture they will inevitably encounter.

Loretta's mother is clear about what she calls the "social benefits" of Bighand School. As noted in Chapter 4, Loretta transferred the middle of her 6th grade year, after getting into discipline trouble at the elementary school in Sparta. Nancy was deeply concerned about Loretta's peers as bad influences and that Loretta was becoming "a bad girl" and implied that she was sexually active and that she smoked. She was worried about the preoccupations of early adolescent culture and its corrosive values. When I asked

Nancy to describe the distinction she saw between Bighand School and Sparta Middle School (from which Loretta transferred) and what kids learn there, she responded emotionally that children at Bighand are:

> much less self-absorbed, I would say, much less preoccupied with how they look. I mean, I can just think of, say the girls here, they probably have chores... Where city kids, they go home from school, and they read Teen Magazine or Young Miss and watch a lot of television and are just much more caught up with what's popular rather than just [the] functioning of life. A big difference. And with that I think the country kids are a lot kinder. Just the way, and I'm not trying to make it sound like they're Amish or anything, but I think they do just live a different life and just have more kindness, and you learn to be kinder and maybe stay out of trouble. And the kids here [at Big-hand] have to get their work done or else.

There is a tone of desperation to Nancy's words. Not all parents state as strongly as she does their concern for youth culture. For example, Kim and Daisy are transferring to middle school and their parents, while acknowledging the troubling aspects of youth culture, say their children can withstand it. Nancy, who was an unwed mother when Loretta was born and now an anti-abortion activist, is in many ways operating on stereotype (that country girls have "chores") and she has limited knowledge of the internal working of the school, like most Bighand parents. Nevertheless, she is clear about what she believes is the insulating effect of Bighand School to youth culture.

Defending Community and a Way of Life

A capacity for Bighand's students to cope with youth culture and the community's confidence in their secondary school success, provided by and epitomized by Mrs. Hoffman "classes," take on further symbolic meaning in this country school. The late 1990s has presented rural America, and rural Nebraska in particular, with another farm crisis. Commodity prices have bottomed out. In particular 1998 saw a widespread and rapid wave of consolidation of small family farms into bigger farms and bigger agribusiness entities (Drabenstott, 1999). This economic trend has been underway for some time, but the current rapidity of consolidation is "producing [social] geographic shifts and dramatically changing agriculture's linkages to local communities" (Drabenstott, 1999, p. 71). Consequently, rural farming communities are experiencing more intensely a sense of a siege from the larger society and economy.

Add to this Bighand's school board members' complaints that the Nebraska State Department of Education continues to add confusing rules and regulations for the Class One schools to follow and that the neighboring school districts, particularly Sparta-Johnville, want them to close down to appropriate their property tax revenues for school funding. Even the community's own unicameral state senator, who is a farmer and understood as a pro-farm and pro-rural politician and well liked in the Bighand community, does not hide his disdain for small country schools nor his strong belief in school consolidation. As the exasperated school board secretary said during a board meeting on a dreary February night, "They want to make it hard for us to hang on."

There seems to be an air of resignation in the Bighand community that the family farm and the small farming communities are on the wane, never to recover. Molly's father was one of those who left farming in the crises of 1980s. In this subtly shared sentiment, only those big and strong enough can, and ought, to survive. This seems representative of a general sentiment across the State. According to Chuck Hassebrook, director of the Center for Rural Affairs Nebraska-based rural advocacy and research organization, and a regent for the University of Nebraska, many farmers in the State seem to accept as inevitable the passing of the family farm and with it "a way of life" (personal communication, 1999).

Yet, the Bighand community is hanging on to its school at a time when it would be just as convenient for them to close and send its children to the affiliated school districts. Some families who reside in the district do this already precisely because their children will ultimately attend and finish school in these districts and want them acclimated to the schools. But for those who continue to put their children at Bighand, this can be seen symbolically as a way to inculcate some values they hold dear that are rural or agricultural—part of the way of life that is under siege and on the wane. These values appear to be what they want their kids to have as they enter large graded middle and secondary schools, over which they feel they have no influence or control and is composed of youth culture of which they are deeply suspicious. Country schooling, in this community and at Bighand School, conceivably symbolizes a defense of the community and a way of life from social and economic siege.

When viewed against these larger socio-cultural and economic features, the values of independence, hard work, following through, and self-discipline, take on a deeper hue. Moreover, the primary role of Mrs. Hoffman's modern recitation instruction of socializing children into these takes on a complexity of which I suspect even she is unaware. This recitation takes on deep symbolic values as a local cultural, cultural practice in a traditional institution. It is easy to criticize school practices when viewed free from culture, history and contemporary politics and economics.

UPPER RILL SCHOOL:
EMERGENT PROGRESSIVE PEDAGOGY

Mrs. Hoffman's teaching is tightly woven within the fabric of Bighand community and rural life. These render her recitation-based pedagogy sensible, despite the potential to criticize her practices as insupportable. Will Tomlinson's teaching happens practically in spite of similar community circumstances. His practices, exemplified by Junior Great Books, have emergent, "progressive" properties, that grow out of Will's personal desire to teach in more ambitious ways that he sees removed from any larger reform effort in literacy or literature. Will's practice resembles the kind of ambitious instruction called for by reformers (see Cohen & Hill, 2001). The place of conversation and the importance of student ideas and points of view, that are strongly evident in the Junior Great Books conversations and implicit in Will's commitment to "thinking," represent a kind of teaching that alters substantially conventional teaching practice and the relationship between students, teacher and subject matter. Will's teaching practices are progressive in the sense that they take children and their ideas seriously and as valid starting points for instruction, the kind of "meeting of the minds" that Will calls this kind of teaching.

If Will Tomlinson is effectively shielded from the kinds of widely distributed values and expectations that shape and reinforce Mrs. Hoffman's pedagogy, and if such shielding permits him to imagine and enact some more ambitious teaching, exemplified by JGB, is there anything more that can be said about Will's teaching other than he has found himself in a setting that lets him teach in these ways?

What is significant, in my view, is that his practices occur in the absence of any kind of intervention or external incentive. They grow out of Will's personal desire to teach in new ways and in ways that make sense to him. He makes little or no reference to his own teacher education as an important source of his current views on curriculum and teaching. He pursued JGB on his own and the workshop he attended was not part of the numerous in-service activities that are available to him in his Educational Service Unit. Cal did not ask him to do JGB, or to take on any new reading or literature program for that matter. These practices comprise only part of Will's overall teaching and in this regard Will has much in common with many teachers who create hybrids with teacher- and textbook-centered instruction. Like Mrs. Hoffman, he has a charge to ensure and demonstrate that his students are at grade level. But he is not explicitly expected to accomplish this via textbooks, though he does use them as pragmatic devices. More importantly, "getting through" a standardized curriculum is only part of his teaching goals. And this is effectively a compromise for him. Will has the opportunity afforded by his teaching setting to aspire to something more than this in working toward getting his students to think.

Buffering Community Expectations

Will is able to do this for two primary reasons. First, and as I outlined in Chapter 5, Will has the confidence and support of his principal, Cal Booker. Cal presents Will with a great deal of autonomy to teach in ways he wants to, as long as he lives up to his end of the implied bargain that Will demonstrate that students are at grade level. The kinds of expectations communicated by and enforced through the Bighand School administrators are effectively kept at bay by Cal. Whereas Bighand administrators presume the usage of textbooks to achieve this, Cal demonstrates his value of teacher autonomy to decide how "being at grade level" is demonstrated. While Will does use textbook series to achieve this, Cal does not presume he will use them to do this. Moreover, Cal views this autonomy as the key to making one-teacher schools valuable institutions. Over the five years of Will's teaching tenure at Upper Rill, his autonomy has become part of the teaching fabric of the school. Will bristles when he believes he is getting signals that he needs to collaborate with other Class One teachers to coordinate curriculum for things like state standards. As he jokes, "I do not work well with others."

I should note that one kind of community expectation does make its way into Upper Rill and finds harmony with Will and his practice. This has to do with demonstration of "discipline." The School board treasurer, a successful farmer whose farm lies kitty corner to the school and who is well known and well respected in the community, confided in me that he feels the appearance of order at the school is very important. "We cannot have it look like the inmates are running the asylum," he said with a hearty laugh, while recognizing near absurdity of this as an expectation. "Of course," he says, "there are more important things than making it seem like kids are not making trouble, but people want to know that things are under control."

This preoccupation with order in an modern agricultural community with German ancestry is worthy of a sociological study itself. But for purposes of this analysis it is important to point out the visible outcome of Will's extraordinary and subtle social control at the school appears as a strong disciplined environment to parents and community members. I think Will's gender plays into this in no small measure. Consequently, Will does not view the expectation of discipline as an expectation because it fits so well with what he accomplishes as a matter of course.

The second primary reason for Will's buffering from a strong expectation of traditional teaching in a country school is much less external to Will. It has to do with his own personal experience. "There is nothing rural about me," Will declared when I first met him. "I teach in a country school, but I wasn't a country kid like these kids here." Unlike Mrs. Hoffman, Will has had no direct experience as a student, nor as a pre-service teacher, in country schools. He does not reside in the Upper Rill community, nor has he lived in one like it. His job before becoming a teacher was a railroad brakeman, an industrial and decidedly "blue collar" job. He doesn't view one-teacher schools as traditional institutions and does not, even implicitly, see himself as being part of any country school teaching tradition the way Mrs. Hoffman sees herself. His embodied school experience is in large, graded town schools in United. He simply does not understand himself as part of larger the fabric of rural education or rural life.

Moreover, within and from his own experience, Will carries a working, though unarticulated, critique of that kind of graded schooling and the mindlessness that he interprets happening in these schools. Thus while Will does view himself in some sense as a learner and ready to take on new forms of pedagogy, like the Junior Great Books, he also resists a good deal of his own teacher education that he sees playing a role in status quo teaching (e.g., fixation on lesson plans). Hence he questions his own experience, his own teacher education and the general culture of teaching (in both graded and other one-teacher schools) against his value and goal of getting kids to think. It is not the highly organized critique of the consciously "progressive" teacher. He does not speak of, for instance, "habits of mind," "knowledge construction" or the importance of student "sensemaking" or "intentionality." But this is critique nonetheless. It helps Will take a stand on wanting students to learn how to think; he does not want his students to be or appear "stupid" and, simply put, not be able to think.

The practical consequence of these buffers is that Will retains authoritative autonomy over his practice in way that Mrs. Hoffman does not. This control is concrete in his freedom from administrative restraint; it is subjective and symbolic in his own mind. Consequently, he persistently views the school as a place of opportunity to try out new practices. He understands the potential risk that might accrue if he did not have such control and the support of his principal. He informs that he sees teachers in other Class One schools preoccupied with new assessment and accountability schemes and the Nebraska State Standards. He feels some pressure to deal with them. And Will knows teachers in United who are anxious about similar things. Cal's approach to dealing with such pressures, and to helping Will deal with them, is to do the minimum of what is expected, "So that we cannot be accused of ignoring policies. Do these well, and get them off our backs. *Then* do the good stuff" (emphasis his).

Taking Risks: Getting it versus Getting Through it

This freedom that Will is afforded—and creates— lets him live comfortably with taking on new teaching practices and with the tension that these create with ensuring that students are at grade level. In late March, Will and I had the following conversation about his practice, which I have reconstituted from my fieldnotes. I asked him about this freedom he has, the Junior Great Books as epitomizing what he tries to accomplish, and the subsequent tension this creates with having to get students on grade level.

> Steve: When you think of the Great Books, what is it you are trying to accomplish in particular? Why use these books instead of a standard basal like the other Class One teachers you and I know?
>
> TW: I guess I would kind of look at it this way: I know that the kids have to get though their materials for a particular grade they are supposed to be in, and parents should expect that. They need to know. But I really want students to "get it," to be thinking about a story. The Great Books helps do that, I would say. Better than that Houghton-Mifflin crap I had before — know the characters, read the story, answer the questions at the end, fill out some worksheet, take a test and then you are supposed to have read and know a story [rolls his eyes]. You know how I feel about that.
>
> Steve: Too low level? Kids are capable of doing more than that?
>
> TW: Right. They're not stupid.
>
> Steve: You might say that you see it as a matter of having kids "get it" versus "getting through it"?
>
> TW: Yes. Kids "getting" [motions with quotation marks with fingers] the complexity of a story, not just getting them through it.

And when I asked Will about the relationship between his operating philosophy and how it is expressed in the JGB for his literature curriculum, his answer is that this is self-evident. He simply points and waves at the student's desks and calls it "this stuff" and simply refers to it as "older kids looking out for younger kids, helping them with their work" and the "younger kids learning from the older kids."

> Steve: Is this natural to you [to have kids of different ages working on the same tasks]?
>
> TW: Ah, well [laughs], here it is almost essential.

Steve: Aren't you tempted to simply put kids through their text-books and workbooks at their grade levels?

TW: I can see that, and we do some of that. But they'd be missing out on this [points and waves at students desks, referring to the interaction that happens there].

Steve: I can imagine some educators saying that the older kids are not getting ahead when they have to read a younger kid's story. Or a younger kid being frustrated that the story might be over his head.

TW: I know what you're saying. I'm not sure that holds water for me anymore. I think the younger kids benefit from being with the older kids, seeing how they think about things and do their work, learning how to be more mature.

Steve: Is there anything you worry about?

TW: Um. [long pause]. Sometimes I wonder, "What if I'm wrong?" I guess I have them next year if I find out that they've missed out on something.

In this thoughtful and candid moment of reflection, Will is pointing out what has become an kind of ethical dilemma. He sees that at Upper Rill the students have a fluid inclination and clear capacity to work together across age levels. The conversations around *Gaston* and *Wisdom's Wages and Folly's Pay* offers some strong evidence of that. Yet, American school culture is a graded school culture, the "factory model" legacy of mass schooling. Time committed to multiage (across at least seven grade levels at Upper Rill) seems to run up against a standardized, "graded appropriate" curriculum as organized in textbooks, testing and district promotion policies. This leaves Will with some nagging doubts—*What if I'm wrong?*

I believe that Will is dealing with competing senses of what it means to be good to students *in this setting*. He has his immediate experience with these children and then of what the larger school world says is important. One of the ways that he is able to cope with this in day-to-day fashion is that he has no totalizing graded school culture around him communicating institutional-wide expectations about standardization. He is splendidly isolated. Moreover, the students' parents are uniform in their satisfaction that he is maintaining discipline (a key value for them) and that their children are learning, and so is his principal. Not only can he cope because the school is small, he also has students the following year and feels that he can make up for whatever deficiencies a student may have. This reflects the kind of comfort and control he has over curriculum and students that allow him to create a conversation-based curriculum using resources like Junior Great Books.

NOTES

1. The Metropolitan Achievement Test at Upper Rill and Iowa Test of basic Skills at Bighand for the years I was collecting data.
2. See Geertz's (1973b) discussion of religion as cultural models and the distinction between models of and models for.
3. He would not allow me to examine the scores due to his concern for confidentiality. I take him at his word that the scores are what he says; he is known as a scrupulously honest person.
4. Some thought I was implicitly enlisted to tell the story of their school's success; just as some thought I would provide public data critical of Mrs. Hoffman. Many were disappointed when insisted on confidentiality, including Molly's mother who wanted the "good news" about the school and David and Kimberly's mother (and the board president's wife) who assumed that I would tell the "bad news" about Mrs. Hoffman.

REFERENCES

Cohen, D. K. (1988). Teaching practice: Plus ça change... In P. W. Jackson (Ed.), *Contributing to educational change: Perspectives on research and practice* (pp. 27–84). Berkeley, CA: McCutcheon.

Cohen, D.K., & Hill, H. (2001). *Learning policy: When state education reform works.* New Haven: Yale University Press.

Cuban, L. (1994). *How teachers taught: Constancy and change in American classrooms.* New York: Teachers College Press.

Drabenstott, M. (1999). Consolidation in U.S. agriculture: The new rural landscape and public policy. *Federal Reserve Bank of Kansas City Economic Review,* 1st Quarter.

Elmore, R. F., Peterson. P., & McCarthey, S. J. (1996). *Restructuring in the classroom: Teaching, learning, and school organization.* San Francisco: Jossey-Bass.

Geertz, C. (1973b). *Religion as a cultural system. The interpretation of cultures.* New York: Basic Books.

Swidler, S.A. (2000). Notes on a country school tradition: The recitation as an individual strategy. *Journal of Research in Rural Education, 16*(1), 8–21.

Theobald, P., & Nachtigal. P. (1995). Culture, community, and the promise of rural education. *Phi-Delta-Kappan, 77*(2), 132–135.

CHAPTER 7

ONE-TEACHER SCHOOLS, SCHOOL SIZE AND REFORM

What do Upper Rill and Bighand Schools have to say to us about instructional reform, school size and enhancing the intellectual lives of children in rural and non-rural schools, as individual cases and when contrasted? If I am in any way accurate in my claims that Mrs. Hoffman maintains a traditional, conservative pedagogy that is rational in its school and community setting, and that Teacher Will's instruction has emergent properties of progressive teaching, then this would seem to expand, and complicate, our understanding of school size and its place in the improvement of instruction.

At a base level, this comparative ethnographic study indicates that school size is hardly a cause or, in quantitative terms, an independent variable that in any way guarantees high quality teaching and, therefore, student academic engagement and learning. Rather, small school size is a factor that *enables* the more ambitious kinds of instruction that Will takes on.[1] Conversely, it can also act as a factor that maintains certain kinds of teaching and confines practice to the recitation.

Taken by itself, one might claim that Upper Rill School is a shining example of the one-teacher school. We might theoretically and optimistically generalize that all teachers will naturally exploit their small scale, multi-age settings to engage, or at least aspire to, high quality instruction that is geared toward getting students to think. However, with Bighand

Naturally Small: Teaching and Learning in the Last of the One-Room Schools, pages 113–118
Copyright © 2004 by Information Age Publishing

School we can see that when a small country school is intertwined with a community's value matrix, and has a conscientious teacher who nevertheless has no image nor incentive for altering her orientation toward knowledge, student learning and the practices that can accommodate these, small school size can effectively inhibit change. In terms of improving teaching practices, the case of Bighand School indicates the small scale setting can be a limiting feature. Conversely, the case of Upper Rill shows how such settings can be liberating to a teacher who imagines and desires "something better."

This comparative study contributes to the view that simply making big schools small or making new small schools is by itself no policy panacea (Lee & Smith, 1996; Raywid, 1997). Smallness can be limiting *or* liberating, depending on how it is viewed, construed and used by practitioners, their administrators and, in no unimportant way, the community in which a school resides. This brings into relief at least two important issues for the improvement of teaching and the intellectual lives of children. One is directed generally at small school reform and the other toward rural schooling and community-based education.

SMALL SCHOOL CHANGE: TEACHERS, STUDENTS AND KNOWLEDGE

The comparison of Bighand and Upper Rill Schools indicates that any robust change in practice in a small school requires a concurrent change in a teacher's conception of the nature of knowledge and the roles of both the teacher and student in relationship to knowledge, what Elmore (1996) calls the core of all teaching and teaching reform. In this way, the challenge of changing teaching practices in a small school is hardly different than it is in a large, graded schools. These are fundamental questions that are beyond simply acquisition of a new textbook series or even taking on a new kind of curricular program altogether, such as the Junior Great Books. If teaching is conceived as merely the transmission of discrete bits of information, handed out by the teacher, via textbooks and workbooks, to be digested by students and tested for and recorded as student achievement, then size of the school is nearly irrelevant to a change in teaching. The size of the school may lead teachers to rationally create systems of conservative instruction if they retain this restricted view of knowledge and are required to follow the directive of "getting through" a fixed curriculum. This kind of instruction can be, and has been, carried out just as efficiently and effectively in large schools as it can in small schools (Cuban, 1994). In a sense, one could say that *any* kind of teaching is easier to achieve in a small setting.

The case of Teacher Will shows a teacher's disposition to take on robust teaching and curriculum innovations and make them his own. In some ways he carries a more robust notion of knowledge—getting students to think—and he views his small setting as an opportunity to take risks. He does not have an articulated view of knowledge. However, if we take his view in light of his teaching actions, we can see his more robust notion of knowledge come to life. If we would like for a teacher like Mrs. Hoffman, who has a great deal of experience *and* success in her system of "classes," for her to alter her practices—so as to make children's ideas more central, to consider knowledge creation over knowledge transmission, to have students demonstrate learning in more "authentic" ways, to create interdisciplinary projects and to have children across ages work together in a self-conscious community of learners—then Mrs. Hoffman has a formidable challenge in front of her. The support she needs for her own learning, professional development and autonomy is just the same as a teacher in large and graded school whom we would want to take on more risks for ambitious teaching. The role of a supportive administrator who can strike a decent bargain with a teacher and grant autonomy seems invaluable in this regard.

I think it is utterly misguided to simply say that a teacher like Mrs. Hoffman needs to be replaced, as many educators suggest when I discuss Bighand School with them. Their reactions are to the more superficial aspects of her practices that are not too terribly appealing, especially from the student's point of view. But, this fundamentally misconstrues and gravely underestimates the role her teaching plays concretely in the school *and* symbolically in the community. Moreover, it is disrespectful to the community and to Mrs. Hoffman, who is doing effectively what is expected of her. Most importantly, this would not solve the larger problems in the larger culture of conservative teaching that inhibit effective change and the powerful local expectations for a teacher in a school like Bighand. To make for effective change in instruction, and the intellectual lives of students, it is not enough to simply make schools smaller; chances are little would change.

THOUGHTS ON RURAL SCHOOL REFORM

Rural educators are correct to raise their eyebrows when urban school reformers claim to be innovating small scale schooling. The one-teacher school remains *the* rural educational institution. As Mrs. Hoffman told me upon hearing of the urban small schools movement, "We've had small all along." I think that rural educators stand much to gain from retaining, and perhaps re-creating, their small schools. Teacher Will's work suggests that great things are possible in small, rural schools. Mrs. Hoffman's teaching informs us that small schools like hers exert a powerful symbolic connection to community and an agrarian way of life. While Mrs. Hoffman's teaching is susceptible to legitimate *educational* criticism, in view of what most teacher educators advance and reformers are seeking to encourage, Teacher Will's practice inheres no deep symbolic connection to place or community and may possibly inhibit it.

Some rural educational reformers eloquently claim that small, rural schools' connections to their communities are their greatest resource for curriculum development (Theobald & Nachtigal, 1995). "Place-based" education is in the vanguard of rural education reform. The deliberate and conscientious use of local culture, history and natural environments is advocated as counterweight to the decontextualized, universalized curriculum that erodes students' "sense of place" and their own rural identities (Haas & Nachtigal, 1998). This exerts a powerful pull on rural educators who see the effects upon their students of the disintegration of local economies, traditional institutional structures and communities.

Yet rural educators are not immune to the problems of improving instructional quality. I think it is utterly mistaken to simply assume that because rural schools are small that they have somehow, by definition, higher quality instruction than their urban counterparts. First of all, there is simply no evidence that the quality of *instruction* in rural schools is any higher than in urban schools. Moreover, too much plays into school success and failure than poor instruction. Teachers in poverty-stricken rural communities know this all too well. I think we can safely assume that most reformers, rural or urban, would respectfully discourage the teacher-centered, textbook-bound, and intellectually limited instruction that takes place at a school like Bighand. Exclusive use of recitations may be effective, but this hardly makes for lively academic environments.

The case of Bighand School would indicate that the task of changing school practices is challenging. Mrs. Hoffman's teaching is deeply and symbolically connected to Bighand's community's values and fears and she has every reason to conclude that she is correct in her practices. I cannot conclude that she is a poor teacher. Moreover, the case of Upper Rill raises some provocative and not altogether comforting questions when we think of schools' connections to community. Teacher Will is effectively isolated from the kinds of expectations that are interwoven in Bighand School. Bighand School's community connection and Upper Rill's relative isolation would seem to undermine at least part of the premise of "place-based" reform ideas.

This raises some thorny questions for the rural school reformer: Does a small school actually need to be isolated from its community in order to permit a teacher to take on more ambitious practices? Is change possible at

Bighand School when there is an array of cultural values to keep things the way they are? How deeply should we respect curriculum and teaching traditions in rural schools and communities? What these questions point to is a formidable reform task: that if there is "something better" in terms of instruction, communities themselves must be educated and willing to transform their expectations for and images of good teaching so that assiduous teachers like Mrs. Hoffman can transform their practices. Why should a teacher like her change her practice and risk creating disruption in a community value system?

CONCLUDING REMARKS

If anything, this book offers portraits of teaching in the last of our one-teacher schools. It is my hope that these portraits leave some impression of the complexity of teaching and the utter coherence and symbolic values that teaching practices can have, even those we may ultimately conclude are not desirable. The coherence of teaching practices also point to the complexity of changing them. In each school that I studied, what came so simply and naturally to the teachers belies a complexity I think escapes even their own consciousness.

Mrs. Hoffman's recitation system is indeed elegant in its efficiency. That it happens so routinely masks the particular knowledge needed to carry out *this kind of recitation instruction.* We must bear in mind the kind of knowledge and skill it takes to teach the way she does as we edge toward asking teachers to modify practices like hers. Mrs. Hoffman is capable of complicated teacher thinking. That her teaching connects so deeply to the school's community's values would point to a great deal of un-learning *and* a need to persuade a community that there might be, in Will's words, "something better."

In many ways this reveals the problem of all public education reforms: a need to persuade a critical mass of constituents that something needs changing *and* that change can happen. I think we learn from Upper Rill, Teacher Will, and his principal Cal Booker, that this critical mass is so small, when compared to any large graded school and consolidated school district, that envisioning substantial change is not so far fetched, or as daunting, as I first suggest. Consolidation, to pick one policy, increases the critical mass and therefore this challenge to change.

And this is what I think we can see at Upper Rill. Will's conversation-based pedagogy comes just as easily to him as the recitation comes to Mrs. Hoffman. He seems almost perplexed when I tell him what he does is rather remarkable in the big current and historical schemes of teaching practices. His modesty masks the complexity of teaching and his own learning needed to make it happen. Will calls himself an ordinary teacher. If we take him at his word, then what this study shows that, in the right circumstances, an ordinary teacher can do extraordinary things.

NOTES

1.   I am grateful to David Cohen for pointing me in the direction of viewing small schools as enabling resources rather than causal structures.

REFERENCES

Cuban, L. (1994). *How teachers taught: Constancy and change in American classrooms.* New York: Teachers College Press.

Elmore, R. F. (1996). Getting down to scale with good educational practice. *Harvard Educational Review, 66*(1), 1–26.

Haas, T., & Nachtigal, P. (1998). *Place value: An educator's guide to literature on rural lifeways, environments, and purposes of education.* Eric Clearinghouse/Rural Education and Small Schools

Lee, V., & Smith, J. B. (1999). Social support and achievement for young adolescents in Chicago: The role of academic press. *American Education Research Journal, 36,* 907–945.

Raywid, M.A. (1996). The Wadleigh Complex: A dream that soured. In B. Boyd, B. Crowson, & H. Mawhinney, (Eds.), *The politics of education and then new institutionalism: Reinventing the American school* (pp. 101–114). Philadelphia: Falmer.

Theobald, P., & Nachtigal. P. (1995). Culture, community, and the promise of rural education. *Phi-Delta-Kappan, 77*(2), 132–135.

LaVergne, TN USA
08 April 2011
223476LV00002B/82/A